G000093800

ROCK 'N' ROLL MOVIES

QUICK TAKES: MOVIES AND POPULAR CULTURE

Quick Takes: Movies and Popular Culture is a series offering succinct overviews and high-quality writing on cutting-edge themes and issues in film studies. Authors offer both fresh perspectives on new areas of inquiry and original takes on established topics.

SERIES EDITORS

Gwendolyn Audrey Foster is Willa Cather Professor of English, and she teaches film studies in the Department of English at the University of Nebraska, Lincoln.

Wheeler Winston Dixon is the James Ryan Endowed Professor of Film Studies and Professor of English at the University of Nebraska, Lincoln.

Steven Gerrard, *The Modern British Horror Film*
Daniel Herbert, *Film Remakes and Franchises*
Ian Olney, *Zombie Cinema*
Valérie K. Orlando, *New African Cinema*
Steven Shaviro, *Digital Music Videos*
David Sterritt, *Rock 'n' Roll Movies*
John Wills, *Disney Culture*

● ● ● ● ● ● ● ● ● ● ● ● ● ● ● ● ●

Rock 'n' Roll
Movies

● ● ● ● ● ● ● ● ● ● ● ● ● ● ● ● ●

DAVID STERRITT

RUTGERS UNIVERSITY PRESS

New Brunswick, Camden, and Newark, New Jersey, and London

Library of Congress Cataloging-in-Publication Data
Names: Sterritt, David author.
Title: Rock 'n' roll movies / David Sterritt.
Description: New Brunswick : Rutgers University Press, 2017. |
Series: Quick takes: movies and popular culture |
Includes bibliographical references and index.
Identifiers: LCCN 2017016370 (print) | LCCN 2017032589 (ebook) |
ISBN 9780813583235 (E-pub) | ISBN 9780813583242 (Web PDF) |
ISBN 9780813590073 (cloth : alk. paper) |
ISBN 9780813583228 (pbk. : alk. paper)
Subjects: LCSH: Rock films—United States—History—
20th century.
Classification: LCC PN1995.9.M86 (ebook) |
LCC PN1995.9.M86 S75 2017 (print) |
DDC 791.43/6578—dc23
LC record available at https://lccn.loc.gov/2017016370

A British Cataloging-in-Publication record for this book is
available from the British Library.

∞ The paper used in this publication meets the requirements
of the American National Standard for Information Sciences—
Permanence of Paper for Printed Library Materials, ANSI
Z39.48-1992.

www.rutgersuniversitypress.org

Manufactured in the United States of America

TO MIKITA

AND JEREMY AND TANYA

AND CRAIG AND KIM

(AND OLIVER)

CONTENTS

ROCK 'N' ROLL MOVIES

INTRODUCTION

Since the first appearance of rock 'n' roll movies in the 1950s, they have fired the public imagination, offering images of youthful rebellion, excess, and hedonism, sometimes presented as harmless fun and other times seen as an open challenge to mainstream American norms. Like the music they presented, celebrated, and exploited, the most potent of these pictures changed American culture and then world culture with their message of youth-propelled social transformation.

The history of rock 'n' roll movies is more complex than it may seem at first glance. Many were made for no nobler purpose than cashing in on a hot musical fad. But long before Dennis Hopper's *Easy Rider* (1969) became the first film with a wall-to-wall rock soundtrack, trend watchers could tell that "rock 'n' roll [was] here to stay," as Danny & the Juniors sang in 1958, an endlessly quoted rock 'n' roll reference that every writer on the subject has to cite at least once. More important, savvy observers know that rock 'n' roll is supercharged with meaning about the changing values of the paradigm-breaking decades—the deceptively conservative 1950s and boldly rebellious 1960s—when an unprecedented teen ethos, far from monolithic but always identifiable and distinctive, came to the forefront of popular entertainment, music and movies very much included. The teens of the post–World War II era are now middle-aged or beyond, but the ethos of their heyday still rings out. Underpinning my discussion is the multifaceted question of how rock 'n' roll movies transcended their scruffy B-picture beginnings to become an integral—and respectable!—mainstay of modern-day cultural expression, permanently altering the social landscape that surrounds us all.

This book traces the history of rock 'n' roll in its many filmic forms, putting a wide variety of topics before the lens and zooming in for close-ups on noteworthy narrative films, documentaries, animations, shorts, hybrids, crossbreeds, avant-garde meditations, and experimental whatsits, some of them noble or ignoble failures, others fondly remembered or half-forgotten hits. Recognizing that the moving-image media have captured much more rock 'n' roll than a succinct account can chronicle, I take a necessarily selective approach, guided by my critical tastes and personal predilections as well as my wish to cover the field in a fair and representative way. I focus mainly on rock 'n' roll's first three decades for two reasons. First, these were the all-important periods when the music emerged and came of age, and they remain the golden age when giants walked the earth (or duckwalked, in Chuck Berry's case). Second, most present-day listeners are already au courant with recent developments, whereas the early decades are less familiar and more in need of exposition and explication. The weight of my coverage therefore skews toward the 1950s, 1960s, and 1970s.

The first task of a book about rock 'n' roll movies is to ask what we're talking about. Beginning with the "rock 'n' roll" part of the equation, a loose and flexible definition suits the subject at hand. Critics, scholars, and fans have wrangled over the essence of rock music for decades, and the difficulty of defining it is clear from a game attempt by Michael Campbell and James Brody, who write in the first edition of their book *Rock and Roll: An Introduction* (1999) that the term "rock" implies "a certain sound, or range of sounds. It is not classical, or folk, or pop, or jazz, or country. It is rock" (7). This description is an exercise in negative theology or in the logic used by Supreme Court Justice Potter Stewart when he said of hard-core pornography, "I know it when I see it." The writers are more specific when they name "loud guitars, up-front rhythms," and "rough-edged vocals" among the usual ingredients, but the haze returns when they concede that "a lot of rock music has none of these qualities" (7).

In the second edition of Campbell and Brody's book, they focus more crisply on what rock is instead of what it isn't, likening it to an extended family of sounds that can be "vocal or instrumental, soft or loud, acoustic or electric, cobbled together in a garage or generated on a computer," radiating out "in every conceivable direction," and sometimes—as with the Beatles song "Michelle" or Frank Zappa's semiclassical compositions—qualifying as rock simply because rock musicians wrote or recorded it (2). While that description still casts a wide net, it contains reasonably clear clues to rock's fundamental nature. As to the differences between "rock" and "rock 'n' roll," the writers suggest a terminological triad: "rock," referring to music by white performers or played in the style(s) favored by such performers; "rock 'n' roll," referring primarily to the prototypical rock of the 1950s; and "rock era," an all-inclusive label encompassing rock and its subgenres and substyles, from rhythm and blues, soul, reggae, and techno to heavy metal, new wave, and fusions with other traditions such as jazz, Latin music, and musical theater.

I follow a similar strategy, using "rock 'n' roll" for the music's early wave—from the late 1940s to the early 1960s—and "rock" for the more elaborate forms spawned in subsequent years, starting with the British invasion, the psychedelic sound, and the poetic lyrics of Bob Dylan and Paul Simon and continuing through hip-hop to the present day. Regarding orthography, I have always favored the old-fashioned "rock 'n' roll" over such variants as "rock & roll" and "rock-and-roll" and "rock and roll," marginally more dignified though the latter three may be. There is no authoritative dictum on this matter, so I use "rock 'n' roll" because that's how the term sounded to me as a youthful listener of 1010 WINS in the mid-1950s, when the New York disc jockey Alan Freed popularized the alliterative catchphrase.

The other half of my title, "movies," needs only a brief note. I use the word to designate all types of moving-image production, from theatrical features photographed and projected on thirty-five-millimeter film to digital and analog videos, live television broadcasts, computer-generated imagery, and the rest, whether seen in picture palaces, on the internet, or somewhere between. Let a zillion flowers bloom.

1

THE FABULOUS 1950s

Origins tend to be murky, and identifying the first-ever rock 'n' roll movie is a tricky business. The first film to make tentative contact with the music was Richard Brooks's message movie *Blackboard Jungle*, a juvenile-delinquency drama that premiered in March 1955. This isn't a true rock 'n' roll picture, since its nod to the genre is limited to one song: "Rock Around the Clock," performed by Bill Haley and His Comets, whose Decca Records single had been around since 1954. Officially titled "(We're Gonna) Rock Around the Clock," it was the B-side of the disc—the A-side was "Thirteen Women (And Only One Man in Town)," a song with an atom-bomb theme—and sales were disappointing until *Blackboard Jungle* propelled it to international fame. Heard behind the opening titles, reprised without vocals later on, and repeated at the end, it made a major impression on audiences, and four months after the movie opened, it became the first rock 'n' roll disc to reach the top of the *Billboard* pop chart.

BILL BEATS BIX

The overall impact and influence of Brooks's film were similarly strong, enhanced by attacks from educational groups and especially from Claire Booth Luce, the American ambassador to Italy, whose successful effort to keep it out of the Venice Film Festival helped make it "the most highly publicized film on the worldwide market" (Hollinger 5; quoted in Doherty 58). Together with Nicholas Ray's teen melodrama *Rebel Without a Cause*, released seven months later, *Blackboard Jungle* alerted Hollywood to the idea that rebellious youths on the screen held a powerful appeal for money-bearing youths at the ticket window.

"Although purportedly adult films," the cinema historian Thomas Doherty points out, these timely, controversial pictures "offered convincing evidence that teenagers were becoming the most populous segment of the moviegoing audience." And that segment loved the "foreshadowing of the shape of things to come" that occurs in *Blackboard Jungle* when "the kids erupt in an orgy of destruction and play Frisbee with their music instructor's priceless collection of Bix Beiderbecke 78s" (57–58), demanding "some bop" or at least some Frank Sinatra or Joni James, as they trash and smash the teacher's platters. Rock 'n' roll is never named, but the

adolescent vibe is unmistakable: Jazz is dead! Long live
Bill Haley's rocking rhythms!

JUNGLE SAM

Among the producers taking note of these developments—including the additional million dollars that
Blackboard Jungle earned when moralists like Luce raised
its profile—was Sam Katzman, known in the trade as Jungle Sam, so named for the sixteen *Jungle Jim* pictures he
profitably produced between 1948 and 1955. Katzman had
been catering to young spectators since the middle 1940s,
aiming romances and comedies like *Junior Prom* (1946)
and *Betty Co-Ed* (1946) at "Teen Agers" and action serials
like *Captain Video, Master of the Stratosphere* (1951) and
Son of Geronimo: Apache Avenger (1952) at the "cap pistol"
crowd. By the time *Blackboard Jungle* brought rock 'n' roll
to the screen, the cap-gun kids of the 1940s were Teen
Agers, and their demographic was growing fast. As a savvy
producer with an exploitational turn of mind, Katzman
saw an opportunity for a possible killing in the youth market that hadn't even existed a few years earlier.

The result was *Rock Around the Clock*, which premiered
in March 1956, exactly a year after *Blackboard Jungle* tested
the waters. Produced by Katzman, it was directed by
Fred F. Sears, a B-western specialist who had collaborated

with Katzman on the early youthsploitation venture *Teen-Age Crime Wave*, a 1955 release whose promotional tagline, "Out of the Sidewalk Jungle . . . ," revealed the imitative impulse that inspired it. *Rock Around the Clock* is a prime candidate for first-ever rock 'n' roll movie, so it calls for more attention than its actual content might seem to warrant.

Three ideas appear to have animated *Rock Around the Clock*, each reflecting Katzman's eagerness to cash in on what promised to be (and turned out to be) a very new, very hot trend. Idea 1: make the title song of *Blackboard Jungle* into the title of the new picture. Idea 2: double the ante by showcasing the song not once but twice. Idea 3: have the group that made the song a hit on disc and screen, Bill Haley and His Comets, perform it in the picture. There was an Idea 4 as well: present the movie debut of Alan Freed, the hugely popular disc jockey who had given the new musical genre its moniker.

And a word about that moniker: the so-called race records distributed mainly to African American communities between the 1920s and 1940s became known as rhythm-and-blues records when the entertainment trade magazine *Billboard* changed the name of its black-music popularity chart out of deference to readers. Freed was a white radio personality who boldly programmed R&B on his Cleveland show, and in 1952 he borrowed the term "rock 'n' roll" from the lyrics of various blues and jazz songs—where it was a recurring euphemism for sex—and repurposed it as a race-neutral label for the music he spun for a growing army of (mostly white) listeners. He moved to the New York station WINS in 1954 and began presenting rock 'n' roll revues featuring the likes of Fats Domino, Buddy Holly, and Chuck Berry at Brooklyn's Paramount Theatre and elsewhere. For fans, he was a well-known voice but not a familiar face, and Katzman scored a minor coup by recruiting him for rock 'n' roll's first major film.

DISTILLING DISGUST?

Rock Around the Clock chronicles the effort of big-band manager Steve Hollis (Johnny Johnston) to reinvigorate his career by finding an exciting new musical idiom now that jazz's great swing era is winding down. Leaving the small town he calls home, he heads for New York with sidekick Corny LaSalle (Henry Slate), and while traveling, they find Bill Haley and His Comets (playing themselves) in another small town. The rockers and their manager, Lisa Johns (Lisa Gaye), have been languishing in obscurity, notwithstanding the group's fresh sound and its manager's dancing talents. But everyone now heads for New York, where Freed (playing himself) is speedily persuaded to sign the unknowns as the headliners of his next live revue. There is a happy ending for everyone, including the two managers, who unsurprisingly fall in love.

Haley and company perform six numbers in *Rock Around the Clock,* including the million-selling "See You Later, Alligator" and "Razzle Dazzle" as well as the title tune. Among the stellar ancillary acts are the Platters, performing "Only You" and "The Great Pretender," and among the nonstellar ones are Tony Martinez and His Band, doing four numbers, and Freddie Bell and His Bellboys, doing two. Some latter-day commentators have been less than kind to Haley, the top-lined star of rock 'n' roll's first expedition to the big screen; the critic Marshall Crenshaw finds him "pudgy and decidedly stiff" (186), for example, and the film historian Jeff Stafford observes that he is not a "typical rock star" by today's standards. "Hefty, stiff in manner and well past the age of his scream-ing fans," Stafford writes, "he certainly doesn't look hip but his music proves the opposite," sparking a "gyrating frenzy" among the on-screen teens, even though canny moviegoers may notice that all the songs except "Rudy's Rock" are lip-synched to their hit recordings (Stafford).

Some commentators in the 1950s were unkinder still about rock 'n' roll itself. One of them was the legendary Spanish cellist and conductor Pablo Casals, who found it "the distillation of all disgust of our time," and another was

Francis Braceland, a Connecticut psychiatrist. According to a *New York Times* article published in 1956 with the headline "Rock & Roll Called 'Communicable Disease,'" he diagnosed the music as a "cannibalistic and tribalistic" genre that "impels teenagers to wear ducktail haircuts, wear zoot suits, and carry on boisterously at rock & roll affairs" (Fuchs 18). Haley himself spoke up for the positive effects of rock 'n' roll, especially with respect to racial discrimination at a time when radio stations and concert venues were just beginning to program both white and African American performers. While playing for mixed audiences all over the United States, he said, he saw young people sitting "side by side just enjoying, . . . being entertained by white and negro performers sharing the same stage" (Schonberg 10; quoted in Romanowski 211).

Whether on purpose or by default, *Rock Around the Clock* shared the racial-tolerance agenda, placing the all-white Comets and the all-black Platters onto the same screen. This contributed to the atmosphere of social change that led some civic and religious leaders to call for boycotts of the film; their fears were reinforced when trouble broke out in some places where Haley played and some theaters where the movie was shown. A brouhaha at the Palomar Ballroom in San Jose, California, was dubbed a "Rock 'n' Roll Riot" in numerous headlines, for instance, and fights occurred at a Haley concert in the National Guard Armory in Washington, D.C., where the armory's manager opined, "It's that jungle strain that gets 'em all worked up" (Denisoff and Romanowski 32). On the other side of the Atlantic, some towns in England banned the picture after hearing of "agitated" spectators at London showings.

These responses are hard to fathom in the twenty-first century. Everything from Haley's trademark (a "magic curl" dangling over his forehead) to the look of the group—plaid jackets, upright bass, zany stunts like playing while lying on the floor—screams "square" rather than "subversive" today. But to 1950s teens with youth-culture moxie flowing through their veins, *Rock Around the Clock* was as hip as hip could be. It also made lots of money, pulling in $2.4 million within a year, an eightfold return on the meager $300,000 it cost to produce. Thoughts naturally turned to a sequel.

THE PAGEANT OF ART AND CULTURE

Katzman and Sears were busy filmmakers in 1956; the former produced thirteen pictures, and the latter directed nine. Seven of these were joint projects, and after their Latin-flavored fall release *Cha-Cha-Cha Boom!* the duo returned to rock 'n' roll with *Don't Knock the Rock*, a play-it-safe project again featuring Haley, the Comets, and Freed, joined this time by Little Richard, who was soaring to fame on the wings of "Tutti Frutti" and "Long Tall Sally," both million-selling hits. Lesser lights—the Treniers, Dave Appell and the Applejacks—also perform. Haley and company do their usual stunts (they lip-synch with glee, the bassist straddles his bass), and Sears's directing is bare bones at best. At one point, a pipe-smoking father manages to *miss his mouth* when he goes to take a puff; at another point, the camera dollies in for an extended close-up of a teenage girl's backside as Freed and friends watch her dance with her boyfriend through a window.

The plot of *Don't Knock the Rock*, such as it is, centers on the return of the rock musician Arnie Haynes (Alan Dale) to his hometown. The teens greet him with enthusiasm, but wary adults, including Mayor George Bagley (Pierre Watkin) and newspaper columnist Arline MacLaine (Fay Baker), attack him and his music as menaces to youthful wholesomeness. The climax occurs when Freed helps high-school theater buffs put on a "Pageant of Art and Culture" cleverly designed to show that rock 'n' roll is just another benign link in an aesthetic continuum stretching from Renaissance painting and the minuet to once-scandalous dances like the black bottom and the Charleston, in which the elders once indulged with no signs of lasting harm. "We'd like to show . . . the country that rock 'n' roll is a safe and sane dance for all young people," Arnie explains. His mission bears the expected fruit, as did *Don't Knock the Rock*, earning exactly half as much as *Rock Around the Clock*, a smaller sum but still a tidy return on a tiny investment. Freed parlayed anticipation of the film into excitement over a holiday Rock 'n' Roll Show he presented in February 1956 at the Paramount Theatre in Manhattan, where the picture's New York premiere was accompanied by a dozen doo-wop and rhythm-and-blues acts plus a big band conducted (after a fashion) by Freed himself.

These things notwithstanding, Freed's career was soon to wane. He took a painful hit in 1958 when WINS fired him for badly handling a restive Boston audience, and he took a fatal hit in 1959 when WABC fired him for accepting "payola" from record companies to play and plug particular discs on his show. Katzman dabbled further in the pop field by producing Sears's *Calypso Heat Wave* in 1957, Arthur Dreifuss's *Juke Box Rhythm* in 1959, and Oscar Rudolph's *Twist Around the Clock* and *Don't Knock the Twist*—titles that are either shrewd or desperate, depending on your point of view—in 1961 and 1962, respectively, and he made pictures with folk-music, country-and-western, and Elvis Presley hooks in later years; but horror, science fiction, and comedies took up most of energies after the middle 1950s.

Haley kept on playing, with diminishing returns. Some observers see his lackluster presence in *Don't Knock the Rock* and specifically the contrast between his hapless-ness and Little Richard's paradigm-busting power as har-bingers of his decline. "Haley was the ignition for rock 'n' roll," R. Serge Denisoff and William Romanowski accu-rately write (59). "He didn't invent the sound. He merely popularized it [during] a brief, but magical, moment in the evolution of the genre." Rock 'n' roll kept thriving, but the ignition was no longer needed.

Sundry rock 'n' roll musicals followed the formulas of the Katzman pictures in time to come, and other films naturally went in different directions. Summarizing the contributions of such movies to midcentury culture, the film scholar David E. James notes that they "developed the visual depiction of musical performance along with the singers, the fans, the components of the industry, and some of the ethnic and other social forces that rock 'n' roll culture contained, including the consternation it often caused," and they also spotlighted and legitimized new dancing styles by using them as a "visual counter-part to the music" (42). Among the more significant were the following:

- Edward L. Cahn's *Shake, Rattle & Rock!* (1956). Black acts and white acts (but no integrated acts) appear in this picture about a "society" of three or four fogeys—one of them is an undertaker who envisions the people he meets as future corpses ripe for his practice!—who try to have a rock 'n' roll club banned from their community but fail because the club is a terrific place where doing "arts and crafts" keeps teens out of trouble.

- Frank Tashlin's *The Girl Can't Help It* (1956). Like Tashlin's best films with Dean Martin and Jerry Lewis, this over-the-top comedy is cartoonish in its style, sociological in its interests, and satirical in its attitude. The plot centers on a sub–Marilyn Monroe bomb-shell (Jayne Mansfield) whose mobster boyfriend (Edmond O'Brien) hires an alcoholic publicist (Tom Ewell) to make her a pop-singing star despite her apparent lack of talent or training. A number of rock 'n' roll careers—those of Fabian in the 1950s and the Monkees in the 1960s, for instance—have been engineered by behind-the-scenes figures more interested in good looks and potential drawing power than in actual ability to sing or play. The movie plays this syndrome for sarcastic laughs, but Tashlin still taps into the industry's generous resources, juicing up the narrative with performances by currently hot talents. Eating his satirical cake and having it, Tashlin simultaneously sends up, puts down, and capitalizes

on the pop-culture industry in which he was himself a
canny player.

- Roger Corman's *Rock All Night* (1957). This offbeat
  item could almost be a one-act *kammerspiel* by Eugene
  O'Neill. Nearly all of it takes place in a second-rate
  saloon, where the evening's congregants include a
  bartender, an extortionist milking him for payments,
  an unpromising prizefighter and his two-bit manager,
  a rock 'n' roll group and its jive-talking manager, two
  gun-toting thugs, a singer unsure of her talents, and a
  customer who becomes a hero by overwhelming the
  thugs with the sheer unpleasantness of his personality.
  The music, heard primarily in the first half, comes
  from the Platters and also Abby Dalton; the second
  half is bargain-basement melodrama, but Corman
  serves up some effective deep-focus images, aided by
  cinematographer Floyd Crosby, and lends a reason-
  able degree of visual interest to the single-set staging.
- David Lowell Rich's *Senior Prom* (1958) and *Hey
  Boy! Hey Girl!* (1959). The husband-and-wife team
  of singer-trumpeter-bandleader Louis Prima and
  singer Keely Smith starred in a handful of pop-music
  movies after reaching the Top 40 with "That Old
  Black Magic" in 1958. The first is a relatively polished
  but ultimately unmemorable romance featuring such
  decided non–rock 'n' rollers as Mitch Miller, Les

Elgart, and Bob Crosby, who hark more toward the 1940s than the 1950s. The second is a more focused showcase for Prima and Smith themselves. His overheated energy and her cool poise make them a well-matched duo.

PRESLEY'S PICTURES

Among the decade's other services to popular culture, the 1950s gave birth to Elvis Presley as a trailblazing singer, international icon, and rising movie star. He made his 1956 screen debut in Robert D. Webb's western romance *Love Me Tender*, playing Clint Reno, a lad who stayed home to tend the family farm while big brothers Vance (Richard Egan), Brett (William Campbell), and Ray (James Drury) marched off to the Civil War, where they fought for the losing side. Returning four years later, the soldiers learn that Clint is married to Vance's erstwhile girlfriend, Cathy (Debra Paget), thanks to an erroneous report of Vance's death. Adding to the clan's confusion, Vance and company just stole a payroll from a Union train, unaware that the conflict has ended and their haul can no longer be kept as a spoil of war.

Originally called "The Reno Brothers," the film was meant as a launchpad for Presley's acting career. Four songs were included to capitalize on his singing fame, and the picture was retitled when his recording of "Love Me Tender" passed the million-copy mark in advance sales, a first for the record industry. Presley's character gets killed during the climax, surprisingly enough, and to soothe the spirits of teens disappointed at this outcome, a spectral Clint Reno sings a reprise of the title tune at the end. The gentility of that enormous hit was much commented on by Presley skeptics who had believed his abilities were limited to the hard rockabilly beat that powered the likes of "Blue Suede Shoes" and "Hound Dog," two of the 1956 recordings that established and defined his public image. (For other observers, including this one, "Love Me Tender" is perhaps the dullest recording of Presley's early career.)

Music played a larger role in Presley's next three films—Hal Kanter's unmemorable *Loving You* (1957), Richard Thorpe's melodramatic *Jailhouse Rock* (1957), and Michael Curtiz's smartly crafted *King Creole* (1958)—and songs stayed front and center when Presley resumed his screen activities in Norman Taurog's appropriately titled *G.I. Blues* (1960) after his career-interrupting stint as an army draftee. As he entered his next phase, Presley wanted to deepen his skills and broaden his range as an actor. But his manager, Colonel Tom Parker, was more interested in profitable soundtrack songs, regarding the movies themselves as publicity platforms and delivery systems for marketable Presley tunes. The songwriter and record producer Jerry Leiber, explaining why he and his partner, Mike Stoller, stopped working on Presley films after *King Creole*, said the strategy of Presley's handlers was to make "every movie the same": "We could have made fucking history, and those assholes only wanted to make another nickel the same way" (Feeney 55).

The two Presley pictures of 1960 illustrate the situation and its outcome. The lightweight *G.I. Blues* includes almost a dozen Presley songs and was a hit, whereas Hollywood auteur Don Siegel's artistically ambitious *Flaming Star*, starring Presley as a mixed-race man (white father, Native American mother) facing violent bigotry in the old West, featured only two songs and was just moderately successful when it opened a month later. Not surprisingly, most subsequent Presley films did not stint on musical interludes.

Presley's later movies ranged from Philip Dunne's troubled-youth drama *Wild in the Country* (1961), where he made one more effort to play a character with noticeable depth, to George Sidney's race-car comedy *Viva Las Vegas* (1964) and William Graham's musical melodrama *Change of Habit* (1969), the last picture he made before getting fed up with films and returning his focus to the recording studio and the performing stage. He died in 1977 at age forty-two.

THE DAY THE MUSIC DIDN'T DIE

If popular culture had a turning point as the 1950s drew to a close, it came with the February 1959 plane crash that ended the lives of three rock 'n' roll stars: Ritchie Valens, who had starred in Paul Landres's *Go, Johnny, Go!* (1959) after scoring a double-sided hit with the soulful "Donna" and the Latin-inflected "La Bamba" in 1958; the Big Bopper, a disc jockey, songwriter, and performer who became a one-hit wonder with "Chantilly Lace," also in 1958; and Buddy Holly, a trailblazing hero of early rock. Holly's many indelible recordings, some with the Crickets and some as a solo act, extend from "That'll Be the Day" and "Words of Love" in 1957 to "It Doesn't Matter Anymore" and "Peggy Sue Got Married" in 1959. These and many other splendid records left a mark on pop music that retains its luster to this day.

Holly was belatedly memorialized in Steve Rash's fine biopic *The Buddy Holly Story* (1978), featuring Gary Busey's supremely likable performance as Charles Hardin Holly, and Valens received similar treatment in Luis Valdez's bio-pic *La Bamba* (1987), with Lou Diamond Phillips portraying the pioneering Hispanic rocker. In the 1971 song "American Pie," the singer-songwriter Don McLean famously memorialized the 1959 air tragedy as "the day the music died," but he was wrong. The music still lives on.

2

THE SWINGING 1960s

The fabled period known as the 1960s didn't fully assume its most notable characteristics—the rebelliousness against authority, the questioning of received values, the skepticism toward tradition, the bent for radicalism and experimentation—until the decade was about half over. And even then most Americans and Europeans went on living the sorts of ordinary lives that economic growth and technological advances had facilitated, at least for the middle and upper-middle classes, in the years following World War II.

Anyone doubting that the early 1960s were a continuation of the late 1950s has only to look at a movie like William J. Hole Jr.'s *Twist All Night*, a 1961 musical originally titled *The Continental Twist* and released in Britain as *The Young and the Cool*. This was Hollywood's third Louis Prima vehicle, and the only sign that anything had changed since its 1958 and 1959 predecessors is the absence of Keely Smith, who had split with Prima a few months before the film was made. The story centers on two problems facing Prima's character: he's playing in a club where members of a youth group congregate without buying anything, and trouble is brewing in an upstairs "art gallery" where an art-theft scam is headquartered. The movie's music comes almost entirely from Prima and his regular backup crew, Sam Butera and the Witnesses, and the film's most endearing aspect is the endlessly good-humored affection these musicians have for one another. Their warmth and friendliness are infectious, and the picture benefits accordingly.

Rock 'n' roll cinema had spread to Britain by the beginning of the 1960s, and there too the attitude toward life and music remained fundamentally conservative, as a movie like Edmond T. Greville's 1960 *Beat Girl* shows. Released to American theaters as *Wild for Kicks*, it was designed to capitalize on the supposedly scandalous doings of the Beat Generation, the youth movement inspired by the writings of Jack Kerouac and Allen Ginsberg, among others. The movie depicts a "cool chick" and her adventures, decked out with faux-existentialist philosophy expressed in pseudo-hip dialogue. Sample: "Next week, *voom*, up goes the world in smoke, and what's the score? Zero. So now, while it's now, we live it up. Do everything! Feel everything! Strictly for kicks!" Adam

Faith sings several songs composed by John Barry, then at the beginning of his long movie-music career.

Voom or no *voom*, revolution was low on the agenda of rock 'n' roll pictures like these. Outside the movies, however, winds of change were starting to waft over the American scene. In sociopolitical areas, pivotal events included these:

- 1960: Four black students staged a sit-in at a lunch counter in Greensboro, North Carolina, inspiring similar protests in other southern states; the Food and Drug Administration approved the birth-control pill, expanding women's reproductive freedom and spurring the nascent sexual revolution; by a squeak in the popular vote, John F. Kennedy defeated Richard M. Nixon in the presidential election.
- 1961: Outgoing president and former five-star general Dwight D. Eisenhower warned that the armed forces and related defense contractors had become allies in a military-industrial complex that posed a potentially grave threat to American democracy; Kennedy gave the go-ahead for the Bay of Pigs invasion, a failed effort meant to topple the new regime of Cuban president Fidel Castro; the first American soldier died in Vietnam.

- 1962: John Glenn became the first American astronaut to orbit the earth; under extreme duress, the segregated University of Mississippi admitted its first African American student; Kennedy and Soviet leader Nikita Khrushchev faced off in the Cuban Missile Crisis, placing the world on the edge of nuclear war.
- 1963: A ruling by the Supreme Court put an end to required recitations of prayers and Bible passages in public schools; the Reverend Dr. Martin Luther King Jr. delivered his legendary "I Have a Dream" speech to some 250,000 participants at the historic March on Washington; Kennedy was assassinated, and Lyndon B. Johnson assumed the presidency.

Signs of change appeared in popular culture as well. Hugh Hefner greeted 1960 by launching his Playboy Club enterprise in Chicago, and the following year Grove Press published Henry Miller's novel *Tropic of Cancer*, triggering a string of obscenity trials that radically revised American pornography law. Joseph Heller published his extraordinary novel *Catch-22* in 1961, and 1962 brought Andy Warhol's first show of Campbell soup-can paintings. American demographics skewed increasingly toward the young—almost half the country was under eighteen—and by 1963, adolescents were spending more than $20 billion a year on everything from clothes and surfboards to magazines and radios, shelling out $100 million on 45 rpm records alone by the middle of the decade. The ubiquity of television (fifty million sets in 1960) led to the ubiquity of the teen-oriented *American Bandstand* (ABC, 1957–89), famously hosted by Dick Clark, and general-audience shows featured a steadily growing roster of pop stars. Radio adapted quickly to the new era as more and more stations took on rock 'n' roll formats, pitching Top 40 platters with cascades of frenetic patter (Aquila 28).

On the musical front, Joan Baez's self-titled first album arrived in November 1960, auguring the folk-music revival that later sparked the folk-rock subgenre. Berry Gordy set up the Motown label in Detroit, scoring with "Please Mr. Postman" by the Marvelettes and "Shop Around" by the Miracles, both chart-topping hits. Bob Dylan debuted at an open-mike event in Greenwich Village in early 1961, and the Shirelles launched the girl-group phenomenon with "Will You Love Me Tomorrow" in the same year. Dave Brubeck's adventurous album *Take Five* became the first jazz LP to sell more than a million copies, and the album's eponymous single also broke the million mark. Phil Spector developed the "wall of sound" aesthetic that enhanced recordings by the Crystals, the Ronettes, and others from 1963 on.

Hits of this era like "Stand by Me" by Ben E. King and "Hit the Road Jack" by Ray Charles showed the growing mass-audience appeal of rhythm-and-blues idioms, while in the same period, the likes of Jan and Dean and the Beach Boys advanced the conspicuously white styles of surf music and the California sound. As the media scholar Anna Everett notes, "society's embrace of youth music culture signaled a pivotal or vanguard moment in charting visible evidence of the possibility for peaceful coexistence, of sorts, as Black and white youths danced together" and African American musicians gained higher profiles in crossover markets (44). The success of the Marcels' bomp-bomp-ba-bomp version of "Blue Moon" notwithstanding, doo-wop was giving way to Motown, soul, surf music, and the Brill Building sound, but rock 'n' roll remained very much on the ascendant as the 1960s shifted into gear.

CONCERT FILMS

Jazz on a Summer's Day, a documentary about the Newport Jazz Festival filmed by Bert Stern in 1958 and released in 1960, is a leading candidate for the first-ever concert movie, a subgenre that took on great importance in the 1960s. Stern's film focuses mainly on jazz stars like Louis Armstrong, Thelonious Monk, George Shearing, Gerry Mulligan, and Jimmy Giuffre, but its inclusion of rock 'n' roll and crossover talents like Chuck Berry, Ray Charles, and Big Maybelle paved the way for rock 'n' roll to enter the concert-movie arena.

The true rock 'n' roll concert genre was born in 1964 with *The T.A.M.I. Show*, comprising almost two hours of material filmed at two rock events in Santa Monica, California, in October of that year. The initials in the title stand for Teenage Awards Music International, although "Teen Age Music International" was used in some of the original publicity. The picture was directed by Steve Binder, who enlisted his television crew from *The Steve Allen Show* (NBC, 1956–60; ABC, 1961; syndication, 1962–64) to film the concerts using Electronovision, a high-resolution videotape system devised by Bill Sargent, who produced the movie. "Virtually every significant chart act of the day" appears in it, according to the critic Marshall Crenshaw, except the Beatles and the Four Seasons (222).

Hosted by Jan and Dean, as personable a pop duo as the period had to offer, *The T.A.M.I. Show* zips from act to act with commendable speed. Instead of building up to its first top-rank attraction, Chuck Berry, the film kicks off with his renditions of "Johnny B. Goode" and "Maybellene," performed in his usual high-energy style, although he doesn't do his famous duckwalk here. The movie then springs a surprise by segueing directly from Berry doing "Maybellene" to Gerry and the Pacemakers doing the same number—the contrast between Berry's hard-hitting backbeat and the English group's milder Merseybeat is striking—and then alternating between Berry and the Brits in an entertaining back-and-forth.

The rest of the film presents one act at a time, most of them in generously timed segments that allow each of them to stretch out and make an impression. Smokey Robinson and the Miracles sing three songs; Marvin Gaye does four; Lesley Gore does half a dozen; the Beach Boys do a lively set that was deleted from the film (apparently for contractual reasons) until it was restored in 2010; and the superb, hair-helmeted Supremes sing four numbers. Respites from the movie's heavy-hitting star power come in the form of the Barbarians and Billy J. Kramer and the Dakotas.

The T.A.M.I. Show saves its chief showstoppers for last. The penultimate act is James Brown and the Famous Flames, doing "Prisoner of Love," the bluesy "Out of Sight," the perennially crowd-pleasing "Please Please Please," and finally "Night Train," one of the R&B group's first huge crossover hits. During the latter two numbers, Brown does a signature routine, becoming so overwhelmed by sheer ecstatic hipness that he positively seizes up, falling to the floor until a Famous Flame wraps him in a robe and helps him to his feet, whereupon he resumes his song until the same spasm strikes again.

Last but the opposite of least, the Rolling Stones take the stage for six numbers including "Around and Around," the classic "Time Is on My Side," and "It's All Over Now," presenting a good cross section of their then-current stylistic range. Brown had hoped to be the closing act, but the producers evidently felt the Rolling Stones would be a better bet. The order of the acts aside, seeing them back-to-back gives moviegoers a battle of the bands that some regard as a high point in concert-film history.

Both bands were at "career crossroads," writes Crenshaw, who describes the situation well. "The Stones had been causing riots in England for a year but hadn't yet scored a significant US hit single. James Brown was the biggest star in R&B, but he hadn't yet found consistent crossover success." Navigating the crossroads brilliantly, Brown offers "a breathtaking display of bodies in motion and balls-out musical excitement," and the Stones inject "charisma" and "mystique" into a "relentless" presentation that drives the audience into "hysteria" (223). Crenshaw overstates that last point, but the teenage girls who abound in the show's live audience give out plenty of adoring screams and tear-edged wails when Mick Jagger and company arrive. The rock 'n' roll concert-movie genre was definitively launched.

Don't Look Back

Folk music was the focus of Murray Lerner's *Festival*, a 1967 concert film comprising segments shot at the Newport Folk Festival between 1963 and 1965. Its lineup includes traditional folk performers such as Mississippi John Hurt, Brownie McGhee and Sonny Terry, and the Georgia Sea Island Singers; folk-revival stars like Pete Seeger, Joan Baez, Judy Collins, Mimi and Richard Fariña, and Peter, Paul, and Mary; blues musicians like Howlin' Wolf and Son House; and crossover artists like Johnny Cash, the Staple Singers, and Bob Dylan, who played his first rock 'n' roll concert set at Newport in July 1965, accompanied by guitarist Mike Bloomfield and keyboardist Barry Goldberg.

The folkies who booed Dylan at Newport were lying in wait, not taken by surprise, since he already had made his turn to electrified (and electrifying) rock on the album *Bringing It All Back Home*, released four months before his Newport appearance. Still and all, this was a hugely controversial move by a singer and songwriter who had been embraced for the past three years by members of the folk and protest-song communities, many of whom saw his conversion to a rock format as a grave artistic mistake, if not a cynical sellout to audience-pandering commercialism.

By now Dylan had established his career-long pattern of continually refashioning his style, voice, and persona, moving from the folk-revival content of his first album, *Bob Dylan* (1962), to the original songs of *The Freewheelin' Bob Dylan* (1963), the morally passionate protest songs of *The Times They Are A-Changin'* (1964), and the sophisticated love songs of *Another Side of Bob Dylan* (1964) before moving to the rock 'n' roll numbers on the first side of *Bringing It All Back Home*, which contrast with the acoustic numbers on the flip side. He stayed with the electric format for two more albums (*Highway 61 Revisited* in 1965 and *Blonde on Blonde* in 1966), went acoustic again on *John Wesley Harding* (1967), unveiled a mellifluous "new voice" on the country-and-western album *Nashville Skyline* (1969), and proceeded thence through a great number of activities culminating in his Nobel Prize for Literature in 2016.

In addition to Dylan's Newport appearance and first electric albums, he spent part of 1965 on a quick tour of England, zipping through seven cities in eleven days (April 30–May 10) with an all-acoustic repertoire drawn from his second, third, and fourth LPs and the non-electric side of *Bringing It All Back Home*. A companion on the tour was the director and cinematographer D. A. Pennebaker, whose documentary shorts included *Jane* (1962), about the actress Jane Fonda, and *Lambert,*

Hendricks & Co. (1964, known as *Lambert & Co.* in its European release), about the eponymous jazz singers. The idea of a Dylan documentary came from Dylan's manager, Albert Grossman, and although Pennebaker's knowledge of Dylan was limited to hearing "The Times They Are A-Changin'" on the radio, he thought the project would make a career-enhancing follow-up to his film on Dave Lambert and Jon Hendricks; so he packed his customized sync-sound sixteen-millimeter camera and set off with the twenty-three-year-old singer, shooting several performances and a wide assortment of backstage activities and backroom dealings adding up to more than twenty hours of footage (Fear).

The apostrophe-free title of *Dont Look Back* conjures up a line—"She's got everything she needs / She's an artist, she don't look back"—from "She Belongs to Me," the second song on the rock 'n' roll side of *Bringing It All Back Home.* While that association is inevitable for Dylan listeners, Pennebaker has claimed that he didn't know of that lyric at the time, that Dylan was against using a song lyric in the title, and that the words actually come from the African American baseball star Satchel Paige's often-quoted remark, "Don't look back. Something might be gaining on you." Be all this as it may, *Dont Look Back* is among the most recognizable titles in concert-film history, even if its luster has been slightly blurred by the film's rechristening as *Bob Dylan: Dont Look Back* in its latter-day release.

The film begins with its most iconic sequence, showing Dylan in an alley where he displays and discards a series of cue cards bearing words from the song playing on the soundtrack, "Subterranean Homesick Blues," which is also the opening number on *Bringing It All Back Home*. (This is one of the moments borrowed and parodied by the writer-director-star Tim Robbins for *Bob Roberts*, his 1992 political satire.) Other memorable scenes include Dylan schmoozing with the wife of the Lord Mayor of London, who doesn't seem quite sure how important this young man is; Dylan's apparently drunken face-off with an apparently drunken hotel visitor; Grossman's angry face-off with an angry hotel employee; and perhaps most notoriously, Dylan's over-the-top invective aimed at a British writer for *Time* who evidently has no idea how to defend his publication, his profession, or himself. Reviewing the film in 1967, I wrote that it presents "a well-edited, beautifully photographed collage of scenes both on and behind stage," showing Dylan in the past— "with remarkably short hair singing protest songs to a group of Negro farmers in the middle of a cornfield"— and in the present, as when he "types out a new song in a lonely hotel room [with] his friend Joan Baez singing quietly in the background" (Sterritt, "Dylan Scene" 6).

Reconsidered decades later, the movie has its dull points but still deserves its classic status.

On to Monterey

The T.A.M.I. Show was the first rock 'n' roll concert movie, but it was also the last of its kind, at least in terms of the look and demeanor of its many performers. Most of the musicians are decked out with spiffy jackets and ties, and the rest wear tidy shirts and slacks with hardly a wrinkle in sight. The minimelodramas embedded in James Brown's routine are enacted with ritualistic precision, and the other groups spice up their presentations with rhythmic body language and crisply rehearsed dance moves.

Dylan's scruffy appearance in *Dont Look Back* shows how much times had changed in three short years, and *Monterey Pop* emphatically confirmed the difference when it premiered in 1968. Psychedelic flourishes enliven the visuals of *Monterey Pop* here and there—notably when Hugh Masakela, not a particularly psychedelic musician, is onstage—and some of the performers are nattily attired. But most rely on energy and charisma, not neatness and polish, to connect with concertgoers and movie audiences. Jimi Hendrix's florid costuming and Country Joe and the Fish's flower-power facial decorations are the polar opposite of the polite couture in *The T.A.M.I. Show*, as are the spontaneous-looking postures, gestures, and expressions that replace the choreographed moves of the earlier rock-concert film.

Monterey Pop was Pennebaker's first feature after *Dont Look Back*, reflecting an ongoing interest in rock that bore fruit in such future films as *Ziggy Stardust and the Spiders from Mars* (1973), documenting David Bowie's last concert under the Ziggy Stardust rubric; *Jerry Lee Lewis: The Story of Rock & Roll* (1991, directed with Chris Hegedus), a documentary biopic; and *Woodstock Diary* (1994, directed with Hegedus), a TV documentary marking the twenty-fifth anniversary of the most historic rock event of all. Filmed at the three-day Monterey International Pop Music Festival in June 1967, *Monterey Pop* documents the world's first full-fledged rock festival, held a year before the Woodstock extravaganza. According to the film and music critic Armond White, the film was as innovative as the festival it depicted, helping to "reconfigure movie musicals from [the] generic convention of private fantasy familiar from *42nd Street* [1933], *The Red Shoes* [1948], *Singin' in the Rain* [1952], and *The Sound of Music* [1965] to a new genre of musical film based on young adult social ritual." As a paradigm-shifting concert movie, it calls for discussion at length.

The camera crew for *Monterey Pop* included such first-rate professionals as Albert Maysles, Richard Leacock, Nick Proferes, Nick Doob, and Pennebaker himself.

Although the film's main emphasis is on performances rather than audience reactions and behind-the-scenes activities, the initial shots depict audience members gathering, technicians setting up for the show, festival coproducer John Phillips making some sort of arrangement on the phone, and the like. The music starts right away on the soundtrack, however, accompanying these anticipatory images with Scott McKenzie singing "San Francisco (Be Sure to Wear Flowers in Your Hair)," a mild-mannered anthem of the hippie scene, and then the Mamas and the Papas crooning "Creeque Alley," a hit that had peaked on the *Billboard* pop chart just a month before the festival took place.

McKenzie's song includes a catchy lyric—"There's a new generation / With a new explanation / People in motion"—that White sees as the "impetus" for the style of Pennebaker's movie, which aims to "reclaim California rock from the insipid '60s beach party movies and even the exploitative teen flicks of the '50s" by stressing "on-stage personas and the mercurial moments of performance and audience interaction." Audience involvement figures only intermittently in the film, but White's enthusiasm is largely justified.

Performance footage starts when the Mamas and the Papas sing their second number, the place-appropriate "California Dreamin'," the 1965 hit that had put the group onto the pop-culture A list. The documentary continues with Canned Heat, Simon & Garfunkel, the South African–born trumpeter and singer Hugh Masakela, Jefferson Airplane with Grace Slick, Big Brother and the Holding Company with Janis Joplin, Eric Burdon and the Animals, the Who, Country Joe and the Fish, two African American superstar acts—Otis Redding and the Jimi Hendrix Experience—and finally Ravi Shankar, the Indian sitar virtuoso whose association with George Harrison and the Beatles made him a world-class celebrity from the middle 1960s on.

Monterey Pop is a sampler of the festival, not a full documentation thereof. Most acts are shown in relatively short clips, and many who performed onstage— the Grateful Dead, the Byrds, the Paul Butterfield Blues Band, Laura Nyro, Booker T. & the M.G.'s, and others— don't appear in the film. Pennebaker does include some of the era's most celebrated musical hijinks, though. Pete Townshend of the Who smashes his guitar, as he'd been doing at the climax of the group's act since 1964, and Hendrix smashes his Fender Stratocaster after setting it on fire, which he'd done for the first time in a London concert a few months earlier. (The latter stunt is famous but doesn't look so impressive on film, with Hendrix squirting lighter fluid from a dinky yellow tin and starting the flames with a flimsy paper match.)

Pennebaker's directing and editing choices inevitably create winners and losers among the musicians. One winner is Otis Redding, whose tremendous magnetism is boosted further by the camera, which frames him against a spotlight that intermittently whites out the screen, as if his dazzling performance were too much for the movie to contain. Discussing this sequence with me in 1969, Pennebaker said it was "a battle . . . between the camera and Otis," resulting not in a "perfect picture" but rather a "searching quality" that's much more interesting (Sterritt, "Pennebaker"). Another winner is Joplin, whose high-octane singing is intercut with shots of Mamas and Papas star Cass Elliot gazing spellbound in the audience. Among the losers are Country Joe and the Fish, who seem low on vigor and inventiveness; Simon & Garfunkel, a terrific team represented by a single song; and the many musicians who participated in the festival but don't appear in the film at all.

Years later, Pennebaker released two spillover shorts using footage from the Monterey festival: *Jimi Plays Monterey* (1986, directed with Chris Hegedus), which gives an extended view of Hendrix's set prefaced by a voice-over reminiscence from John Phillips of the Mamas and the Papas, and *Shake! Otis at Monterey* (1987, directed with Hegedus and David Dawkins), focusing on Redding's spectacular performance, accompanied by both

Booker T. & the M.G.'s and the Mar-Keys horn section, no less. Pennebaker's contributions to documentary cinema extend far beyond rock 'n' roll, but in the rock-film genre, he is a landmark figure.

ENTER THE BEATLES

The remarkable thing about the reception of Richard Lester's *A Hard Day's Night* when it premiered in 1964 is how near-unanimously favorable it was. Critics who weren't nearly as young as they used to be found the first Beatles movie as pleasurable as did the adolescent and young-adult Beatles fans who constituted its obvious target audience. The *Esquire* critic Dwight MacDonald came out of his often-curmudgeonly shell to deem it "a gay, spontaneous, inventive comedy" and "as good cinema as I have seen for a long time" (400), and the decidedly unhip Bosley Crowther of the *New York Times* called it "a fine conglomeration of madcap clowning in the old Marx Brothers style . . . done with such a dazzling use of camera that it tickles the intellect and electrifies the nerves" ("Four Beatles"). The *Village Voice* reviewer and leading auteur theorist Andrew Sarris hailed it as "the *Citizen Kane* [Orson Welles, 1941] of jukebox musicals, the brilliant crystallization of such diverse cultural particles as the pop movie, rock 'n' roll, *cinema vérité*, the *nouvelle*

vague, free cinema, the affectedly hand-held camera, fren-
zied cutting, the cult of the sexless subadolescent, the
semi-documentary, and studied spontaneity" (*"Hard
Day's Night"* 56). Good feelings reemerged when the picture was reissued in 2000. "The picture is a joy," Stanley
Kauffmann wrote in the *New Republic,* reviewing the re-
release. "The Beatles were and remain endearingly brash,
four Pucks with irresistible songs" (22).

Lester was born in Philadelphia and earned a degree
in clinical psychology at the University of Pennsylvania,
where he enrolled at age fifteen. He entered the television
industry in his late teens, progressed quickly from stage-
hand to director, relocated to London as a young man,
and made his first lasting mark in 1959 with *The Running
Jumping & Standing Still Film,* an eleven-minute exercise
in knockabout surrealism created with the comedy spe-
cialists Peter Sellers and Spike Milligan, with whom Lester had worked on the British television programs *A Show
Called Fred* and *Son of Fred* (both ITV) in 1956. He made
his feature-film debut in 1962 with the jazz-oriented comedy *It's Trad, Dad!* (retitled *Ring-a-Ding Rhythm!* in the
US market) and became a world-class figure with *A Hard
Day's Night.*

A Show Called Fred and its sequel were televisual
successors of *The Goon Show,* a hugely popular and
notoriously anarchic BBC radio program (called *Crazy*

People during its first season) that Sellers and Milligan had starred in from 1951 to 1960. John Lennon once remarked that he and the other Beatles were "sons of *The Goon Show*" and saw themselves as "the extension of that rebellion, in a way," and when a United Artists producer asked the band to suggest a director for their first movie, Paul McCartney responded, "Whoever made that *Running Jumping and Standing Still* film? Who did that? 'Cause it was brilliant," adding later about Lester's comedy, "It was just what we liked, we could relate to the humor wholeheartedly" (Kashner).

The group's other members, George Harrison and Ringo Starr, agreed, and *A Hard Day's Night* became a Richard Lester film. Propelled by Lester's hyperkinetic style, it replaces the kitchen-sink aesthetics and simmering class resentments of earlier British New Wave productions—such as Tony Richardson's *The Loneliness of the Long Distance Runner* and John Schlesinger's *A Kind of Loving*, both released in 1962—with a buoyant, endlessly good-natured view of swinging London, the swinging '60s, and Beatlemania itself, a jet-fueled English juggernaut swooping down on America in the vanguard of the British invasion.

The Beatles had conquered America with the advent of their hit single "I Want to Hold Your Hand" in December 1963, along with glimpses of their act on network TV and a blockbuster promotional campaign preceding their February 1964 arrival in New York for their first American tour and their record-breaking appearance on *The Ed Sullivan Show* (also called *Toast of the Town*; CBS, 1948–71), which pulled in an estimated seventy million viewers. Within a month, their first Capitol Records album, *Meet the Beatles*, became the best-selling LP of all time, and in the first week of April, they held twelve positions on the Top 100 chart, including every one of the top five spots, which were occupied by "Can't Buy Me Love," "Twist and Shout," "She Loves You," "I Want to Hold Your Hand," and "Please Please Me" (Puterbaugh).

A Hard Day's Night debuted in July, parlaying its $560,000 budget into revenues estimated at $11 million by the early 1970s (Walker 241). Its critical and commercial success owed a great deal to the stylistic hybridity and genre-bending spontaneity that Sarris described in his review. The influence of the French New Wave was especially important, since many of Lester's techniques in the film—handheld camerawork, impulsive jump-cut editing, a cavalier attitude toward classical rules of framing, continuity, and narrative logic—were just now entering the cinematic mainstream, thanks to the prominence of groundbreaking works by François Truffaut, Jean-Luc Godard, Éric Rohmer, and other founders of the innovative *nouvelle vague* movement. Lester borrowed freely from this vocabulary, adding his own brand of high-energy comic twists.

Perhaps most surprising from a commercial-film standpoint, *A Hard Day's Night* has almost no story to tell; most of it simply follows the foursome through a fictionalized version of their regular routine—rehearsing songs, dodging fans, talking with the press, dodging more fans, preparing for a TV appearance, dodging still more fans, and finally playing a concert before a mighty horde of smitten teens. A loosely strung narrative emerges only in scenes featuring the main secondary character, McCartney's grandfather John McCartney (Wilfred Brambell), who's traveling with the group and gets into considerably more mischief than they do, even though he's invariably described as a "clean old man" by people who encounter him. At one point, the Beatles have to extract him from a casino, and at another point, he induces Ringo to wander off for some personal time at a highly inopportune moment, leading to a climactic scene in a police station, where Ringo and grandpa are both brought on various petty charges. Another key character is a long-suffering TV director (Victor Spinetti) whose exasperation with a flood of minor irritations is clearly a sly parody aimed at Lester by himself.

Lester ascribed the faux-documentary approach of *A Hard Day's Night* to his recognition that the Beatles were

musicians, not thespians, explaining, "you didn't particularly want acting classes for the four boys while we were
actually filming." Talking, traveling, and hanging out with
the group, he and screenwriter Alun Owen found so much
usable material that, he said, it seemed as if the screenplay
"was writing itself right in front of us," and Lester boosted
the mood of off-the-cuff reality further by keeping multi-
ple cameras on the Beatles whenever possible. The train
scenes were filmed during a real six-day train trip, genuine journalists appear in the press-conference scene, and
shooting the big concert sequence involved six cameras
and hundreds of shrieking teenage fans (Kashner). And,
of course, Beatles songs abound, from "I Wanna Be Your
Man" and "Tell Me Why" to "She Loves You" and the
sprightly title tune.

Help, Help

The critical and commercial success of *A Hard Day's Night*
made a sequel all but obligatory, and *Help!* duly arrived
in 1965. The minimal narrative makes Ringo the posses-
sor of a sacred ring and therefore a sacrificial target of
the sinister Clang, the leader of a mystical cult that can't
seem to do anything right. The picture's working title was
"Eight Arms to Hold You," referring to the Beatles and to
an image of the goddess Kali seen in the film, but Lester
wanted to call it "Help, Help," which turned into *Help!*

around the time the eleven-week shoot was completed. The budget was triple that of *A Hard Day's Night*, allowing for Eastmancolor cinematography and location work in Austria and the Bahamas as well as various English locales.

The remarkable thing about the reception of *Help!* was how near-unanimously disappointed it was; although many critics found things to like, comparisons with *A Hard Day's Night* invariably followed, and just as invariably, they favored the earlier film. *New York Times* reviewer Crowther wrote that nothing in the new picture compared with "that wild ballet of the Beatles racing across a playground" or the "wistful . . . ramble of Ringo across a playground" and concluded that the Beatles themselves had now "just become awfully redundant and . . . dull" ("Singers Romp"). The review in *Time* pointed to the new film's "highly professional, carefully calculated camera work and cutting, plus a story line made out of finely wrought jack-in-the-boxes," but still deemed the group's "all-out try at carving out a new career as a screen team" to be "a failure, for as actors they are still nothing but the Beatles" ("Chase").

The shortcomings of *Help!* have been traced to the circumstances of its making. The actual writing of *Help!* is a blur," coscreenwriter Charles Wood commented later. "I don't remember much about it—it only took me a week, I think." And the circumstances of its making can be traced in part to the transformation of the relatively conservative early 1960s into the relatively radical later 1960s, when psychedelics and self-indulgence came into their own. In brief, the Beatles took to smoking considerable amounts of marijuana, as a diversion and as a way of coping with the boredom of the filmmaking process. Lester learned to shoot as much as possible each day before lunch. "*Help!* was a drag," Lennon recalled. "We were on pot by then and all the best stuff . . . was left on the cutting room floor" (Ingham 198). All this said, the film was a box-office hit, and it contains a number of splendid Beatles songs, including the poignant "You've Got to Hide Your Love Away" and the invigorating "Ticket to Ride" as well as the marvelous title tune.

Let It Be

The Beatles had a three-picture deal with United Artists, and after a couple of offbeat possibilities for the third movie failed to work out—as did the hope that their 1968 animation *Yellow Submarine* would suffice—they fulfilled the contract with the 1970 documentary *Let It Be*, directed by Michael Lindsay-Hogg, who went on to make *The Rolling Stones Rock and Roll Circus* (1996) and concert documentaries with Paul Simon, the Who, and Neil Young as well as many television shows and occasional feature films in other genres. The original idea was to document the making of "Get Back," a back-to-basics album (never completed or released) meant to be "a joyous return to their roots, an attempt to rekindle the simple joy of getting together and making music, which had dissipated as their fame and influence grew," in the words of the Beatles historian Chris Ingham, who has crisply anatomized the problems weighing down the production (209). Components of the project would include three live shows at a London theater, a TV show depicting the rehearsal and recording processes, and a TV special presenting selected segments of the concerts.

McCartney was keen on the plan. Lennon was willing as long as Yoko Ono, by then his constant personal and professional partner, was also on the scene. Harrison was against doing live shows in London, which was an integral part of the project. And Starr would basically "do anything to keep the peace." Suggestions of staging the climactic concert in faraway locations or the Houses of Parliament were scrapped for various reasons, and eventually the show was filmed in London's "cold and cavernous" Twickenham Studios, where the "chilliness of the soundstage . . . is evident and matched by the frostiness that develops between the band as the sessions become more tedious and obviously less productive than they'd hoped." Lennon delivered a withering review of the proceedings, saying that "even the biggest Beatles fan couldn't have sat through those six weeks of misery. . . . It was just a dreadful, dreadful feeling" (Ingham 209–10). For many viewers, the film's only saving grace is the rooftop concert that concludes it.

The multipart "Get Back" project devolved into the theatrical film *Let It Be* when the Beatles decided to give the enormous amount of footage Lindsay-Hogg had shot—more than ninety hours of it—to United Artists, thereby wrapping up their three-picture obligation. Meanwhile, the soundtrack album was mixed by Phil Spector after the foursome rejected versions assembled by Glyn Johns, the recording engineer who got first crack at the sessions (Partridge). By the time the movie and LP emerged from the editing suites, the Beatles were no more, although they did regroup a few months later for *Abbey Road*, an album far better than *Let It Be*. The greatest band of all time had disbanded for good.

Movie critics were generally lukewarm about *Let It Be*. The trade paper *Variety* said it was "relatively innocuous [and] unimaginative," noting that throughout the studio session, "Lennon's wife Yoko Ono is always present—close at hand, silent, not participating, yet somehow distracting Lennon, splitting his attention. The Beatles' past togetherness, the chummy camaraderie, the quickness to seize on a line and build a series of gags, is no longer there" (*"Let It Be"*). Calling the film a bore, a critic for the *Observer* wrote that it is "supposed to show how the Beatles work, but it doesn't. Shot without any design, clumsily edited, uninformative and naive, it would have destroyed a lesser group. Yet, there they are, singing away, charming the pants off the most cynical of pop-music haters" (Palmer). As for the soundtrack album, *Rolling Stone* found fault with both Spector and the group: "Musically, boys, you passed the audition. In terms of having the judgment to avoid either over-producing yourselves or casting the fate of your get-back statement to the most notorious of all over-producers, you didn't" (Mendelsohn).

The Other Beatles Films

The Beatles lent their talents to two additional films between *Help!* and *Let It Be.* The first was the 1967 television movie *Magical Mystery Tour*, conceived by McCartney and intended as a plot-free ramble through the increasingly psychedelic precincts of the group's collective imagination.

The period from late 1965 to the middle of 1967 was pivotal in the group's history, as David E. James points out; with the albums *Rubber Soul, Revolver,* and *Sgt. Pepper's Lonely Hearts Club Band*, they "completed the transition from pop to genuine, if drug-fueled, self-expressivity, from 'rock 'n' roll' to 'rock' and indeed way beyond it," further enabled by their exit from live performance in

August 1966, which allowed them to concentrate on the seemingly unlimited possibilities of the recording studio. McCartney dreamed up *Magical Mystery Tour* as a "televisual equivalent of this transformation" in the one communications medium that the group had not yet conquered (James 161). The idea was for the Beatles and friends to ride through the English countryside on a bus that was both a vehicle for the journey and for visionary episodes devised by the various participants.

The title *Magical Mystery Tour* refers to the "magical" properties of psychedelic consciousness and to an outmoded form of recreation called a "mystery tour," whereby people embark on bus trips to destinations they don't know in advance. For a variety of reasons—two posited by James (162) are the sudden death of Beatles manager Brian Epstein shortly before shooting started and McCartney's limited experience with filmmaking—the production never jelled. Ten hours of footage were boiled down to a fifty-five-minute special shown the day after Christmas in 1967, in black and white, not in color as it was filmed. The result was almost universally disliked.

Although the Beatles managed to rationalize some of the negative reaction in later days, they recognized that the telecast was a resounding failure. John Lennon: "They [the public] thought we were stepping out of our roles. They'd like just to keep us in the cardboard suits that were

designed for us. Whatever image they have for themselves, they're disappointed if we don't fulfill it." Ringo
Starr: "Being British, we thought we'd give it to the BBC,
which in those days was the biggest channel, who showed
it in black and white. We were stupid and they were stupid. It was hated." Paul McCartney: "Was it really as bad
as that? It wasn't the worst programme over Christmas. I
mean, you couldn't call the Queen's speech a gas, either,
could you?" George Harrison: "The press hated it. With
all the success that we had, every time something came
out . . . they'd all try to slam it; because once they've built
you up that high, all they can do is knock you back down
again" (Beatles 274). Maybe so. In any case, the experiment was not repeated.

The idea of a Beatles animation came from King Features Syndicate, an American company that already managed a Beatles comic strip and a Beatles cartoon series
(ABC, 1965–69) presenting brief animations accompanied by Beatles songs. The animated feature was produced by Al Brodax and directed by George Dunning,
both veterans of the TV series. Brodax aspired to emulate
Walt Disney's 1940 classic *Fantasia*, and Dunning saw
this as a chance to make an "experimental film." The art
director was Heinz Edelmann, a Czechoslovakia-born
graphic artist who scrutinized *A Hard Day's Night* to get a
sense of how the Beatles walked, modeled the Chief Blue

Meanie's movements on those of Adolf Hitler in newsreel footage, and worked with more than forty animators and almost 150 technical artists to churn out the fifty thousand drawings that convey the antic plot (Denisoff and Romanowski 146). The action begins when Blue Meanies attack Pepperland with weapons that freeze motion and drain away color (rather as the BBC did in the *Magical Mystery Tour* telecast) and climaxes when the Beatles bring back color, joy, and flowers by embarking in the titular submarine, freeing Sgt. Pepper's Lonely Hearts Club Band from entrapment in an antimusic zone, and inviting the Blue Meanies to become music-loving funsters like themselves. The real, nonanimated Beatles then appear as themselves in a short epilogue.

The producers' deal with the Beatles allowed them to use a dozen of the group's existing songs, to which four new songs were to be added. The Beatles obliged out of duty rather than enthusiasm, and musical director George Martin, who composed the film's orchestral score, said that the new numbers—"Only a Northern Song," "Hey Bulldog," "All Together Now," and "It's All Too Much"— were mediocrities that "scraped the bottom of the Beatle music barrel" (Denisoff and Romanowski 148). Be that as it may, the movie and the soundtrack album were rousing hits, and enough critics loved the picture to keep the Beatles' popularity sailing along.

LATER LESTER

A Hard Day's Night made Richard Lester's name, and the lackluster *Help!* did not unmake it; he remained an active film-industry player until his unexpected retirement in 1991. Between his two Beatles features, he directed *The Knack . . . and How to Get It*, a high-energy farce that won the Palme d'Or at the Cannes International Film Festival in 1965, and two years later, he made the 1967 antiwar satire *How I Won the War*, a misfire featuring John Lennon in his first and last solo acting appearance. Told by Lester that he could be "a very interesting actor" if he chose, Lennon replied, "Yeah, but it's fucking stupid, isn't it?" Waiting for camera and lighting setups between takes irritated him beyond measure, although he used some of the time to write "Strawberry Fields Forever," one of his most celebrated songs (Kashner).

Lester's filmography also includes the Broadway-based comedy *A Funny Thing Happened on the Way to the Forum* (1966) and the stylish swinging-'60s drama *Petulia* (1968). After the failure of his postapocalyptic comedy *The Bed Sitting Room* in 1969, he toned down his French New Wave–inspired experimentalism, which was not wearing well with some critics, such as the previously supportive Sarris, who averred in 1968 that Lester was "the most fragmented director this side of Jean-Luc Godard, and his fragmentation is becoming increasingly irritating" (*American Cinema* 196). His later films include an action-adventure trilogy consisting of *The Three Musketeers* (1973), *The Four Musketeers: Milady's Revenge* (1974), and *Return of the Musketeers* (1989); the superhero sequels *Superman II* (1980) and *Superman III* (1983); and two Beatles-related documentaries, the short biopic *Paul McCartney* and the feature-length *Get Back*, about the Paul McCartney world tour of 1989–90.

Even if *A Hard Day's Night* were Lester's only film, his place in midcentury cultural history would be assured. The great filmmaker Martin Scorsese has called him "one of the key figures of the era," and stating that "the pop musical came of age under Lester's ingenious eye," Sam Kashner notes that the first Beatles movie had a strong influence on subsequent pictures by English bands (the Dave Clark Five, Gerry and the Pacemakers) as well as American works like television's *The Monkees* (NBC, 1966–68) and Todd Haynes's postmodern Bob Dylan epic *I'm Not There* (2007). Lester even received a vellum scroll saluting him as the father of MTV, to which he responded with characteristic wit, calling for a paternity test (Kashner).

LESTER'S LEGACY

The progeny of *A Hard Day's Night* are problematic, as progeny often are. One of the offspring is John Boorman's

1965 romp *Having a Wild Weekend*, called *Catch Us If You Can* in its initial UK release. Instead of playing themselves à la the Beatles in Lester's films or the Monkees in their eponymous TV show, the Dave Clark Five play stunt doubles performing in a series of TV commercials starring a model named Dinah (Barbara Ferris) and designed to promote meat, a commodity that wouldn't seem to need all that much promoting. Fleeing the scene a little like Ringo does in *A Hard Day's Night*, team leader Steve (Dave Clark) runs off with Dinah to an island she's thinking about buying with her modeling money. During their odyssey, they encounter a group of hippie-like squatters, a military contingent conducting war games, and a married couple named Nan (Yootha Joyce) and Guy (Robin Bailey), who collect pop-culture relics from the recent and not-so-recent past. The general mood is gray and wintry, going interestingly against the swinging-'60s grain but not providing a very engaging excursion in its own right. In a review for the *New Yorker*, the critic Pauline Kael said it was "as if pop art had discovered Chekhov—the Three Sisters finally set off for Moscow and along the way discover that there isn't any Moscow," fleeing "urban corruption [to] look for pastoral innocence and solitude" but finding that "the corruption has infected the countryside. It is total." For her, the movie's "aftertaste" is "bittersweet," which she defines as "an old-fashioned word with connotations of sadness, of nostalgia, and perhaps of something one might call truth" ("*Having a Wild Weekend*"). It's hard to imagine a stronger case for this chilly, vaguely dyspeptic little film, which is memorable chiefly as the feature-directing debut of Boorman, who made the vastly more satisfying *Point Blank* just two years later.

Bob Rafelson was another first-time filmmaker when he directed *Head*, but he had already joined coproducer Bert Schneider in creating *The Monkees* (NBC, 1966–68), the TV series manufactured to display the Monkees, the most notoriously manufactured rock 'n' roll group of their time. It all began with a September 1965 advertisement in Hollywood's leading trade publications, *Variety* and the *Hollywood Reporter*, that read in part, "Madness!! Auditions. Folk and Roll Musicians and Singers for acting roles in new TV series. Running Parts for 4 insane boys, 17–21. Want spirited Ben Frank's types. Have courage to work. Must come down for interview." It has been suggested that "come down for interview" was a Beatles-era hint to arrive at the audition without help or hindrance from psychedelic substances (Welch 123).

The outline for *The Monkees* was "written six years before the Beatles existed," Rafelson claimed, rejecting the very idea that *A Hard Day's Night* directly influenced the show. But it's likely that *TV Guide* was on the money when it heralded the show's premiere: "Just as its four leading men [Micky Dolenz, Davy Jones, Michael Nesmith, Peter Tork] are patterned on The Beatles, its production techniques are borrowed in large measure from The Beatles' movies" (Welch 83). This aside, what nobody contested was the fabricated nature of the group, which originated in the aforementioned casting call, not in any prior association among the lads who got the jobs.

The lads were individually qualified for this manner of employment, since Nesmith and Tork were musicians with an aptitude for comedy—before long, Nesmith was writing and producing songs for the show—while Dolenz and Jones were actors with an aptitude for music. In the emerging world of postmodern entertainment, however, the wholly commercial basis for their arranged marriage as a rock band became not a liability but a point of pride, as their self-descriptive song "Ditty Diego—War Chant" demonstrates at the outset of *Head*, their first and only feature film: "You say we're manufactured / To that we all agree / So make your choice and we'll rejoice / In never being free." It may seem anodyne today, but rejoicing in "never being free" was quite a statement in 1968. Take that, flower children!

The professional shortcomings of the group were ably compensated for by the professional know-how of their handlers. *The Monkees* won an Emmy Award for outstanding comedy series of 1967, and the episode "Royal

Flush" brought James Frawley an Emmy for outstanding directorial achievement in comedy. Songs on the early Monkees recordings were written by such hit-making talents as Neil Diamond, the team of Carole King and Gerry Goffin, and the team of Tommy Boyce and Bobby Hart, and the likes of Glen Campbell and Hal Blaine were among their backup musicians. As time passed, they turned into an authentic group, and their artificial origins became irrelevant.

Disdainers of freedom though they were, the four-some recognized their skyrocketing success—in summer 1967 their album *Headquarters* was just behind *Sgt. Pepper's Lonely Hearts Club Band* on the charts—and they demanded more autonomy from Don Kirshner, the show's music coordinator. They prevailed over Kirshner, who later became the musical coordinator for another TV show, *The Archie Show*, where the eponymous rock group consisted of cartoon characters "who ... lacked the power to rebel against their producers," as Mark Deming wittily writes. But the Monkees now discovered creative fault lines among themselves, ratings of the series started to decline, and NBC did not renew it in 1968.

At this point, the Monkees wanted to make a movie anyway, so the creators of their TV show "and a friend, the unknown actor Jack Nicholson, went to Ojai, California, with the four Monkees, where they smoked Hawaiian pot while dictating into a tape recorder" (Greene). Nicholson turned the tapes into the screenplay for *Head*, which went before the camera with Rafelson in the director's chair. It quickly proved to be a failure with critics, a flop with audiences, and a disappointment to Monkees fans everywhere. "The Monkees didn't quite understand what the movie was," Rafelson said later, "and I'm not so sure that Jack and I knew what we were doing" (Greene). The movie is indeed a mess, and the soundtrack album barely broke into the Top 50 on the charts. Tork departed from the group in 1968, Nesmith left a year later, and the remaining two Monkees were unable to sustain the franchise as a duo. The band's dissolution was complete by late 1970, two years after *Head* made its very brief and very unsuccessful voyage through the pop-culture scene.

LONELY BOYS

Compared with the upbeat view of 1960s pop presented by the Beatles and Monkees movies, the 1967 melodrama *Privilege* represented the downside in unmistakably somber terms, going much further than *Having a Wild Weekend* in suggesting that the vast popularity and unabashed commercialism of rock 'n' roll could be harnessed by cynical forces for dystopian ends. Paul Jones, lead singer of the British band Manfred Mann, made his acting debut in *Privilege*, the first theatrical picture directed by Peter Watkins, an aggressively political filmmaker who had won an Academy Award with his faux documentary *The War Game* in 1965 and who went on to such sociologically grounded features as *Edvard Munch* in 1974 and *La Commune (Paris, 1871)* in 2000.

Privilege centers on a fictitious rock star named Steven Shorter, a blandly handsome young man whose accomplishments are unanimously revered by people of every age, socioeconomic status, and ideological orientation. The film doesn't convincingly show the reasons for this adoration—the act Steven performs at the beginning of the film, singing a sadomasochistic lament while handcuffed in a portable prison cell, is bizarre and uncharismatic—but his influence on society is so strong that powerful handlers use it to promote their own interests, which range from specific interventions in the public sphere (for instance, combating an oversupply of apples by urging people to overeat the fruit) to exercises of sheer social engineering that culminate in a campaign to cure Britain of being "apathetic, slack, loose in . . . morality" by means of a new universal slogan: "We will conform!"

The clunkiness of that sub-Orwellian slogan sums up the clunkiness of Watkins's movie, which suffers from its own signs of apathy (Jones's passive, undercooked acting) and slackness (the meandering, unpersuasive narrative).

Its morality is emphatic, though, updating the alarm against media manipulation and pop demagoguery that *A Face in the Crowd*, directed by Elia Kazan from Budd Schulberg's original screenplay, had sounded in 1950s terms exactly ten years earlier. Watkins, evidently seeking a veneer of in-the-moment immediacy for his allegorical yarn, borrowed significant details from *Lonely Boy*, a half-hour documentary about the then-rising career of the pop singer Paul Anka, directed by Wolf Koenig and Roman Kroitor for the National Film Board of Canada in 1963. Whether the careerist crooner of "Diana" (1957) and "Put Your Head on My Shoulder" (1959) and soon-to-be lyricist of Frank Sinatra's 1969 anthem "My Way" was an apt model for the supremely malleable antihero of *Privilege* is dubious, as is the moralistic tenor of *Privilege* as a whole.

AVANT-GARDE ROCK CINEMA: ANGER, CONNER, WARHOL, GODARD

The experimental spirit that strode the world in the second half of the 1960s gave rise to a vigorous wave of avant-garde filmmaking in the United States and elsewhere, and in some cases, its practitioners engaged directly with the ambiences and aesthetics of rock 'n' roll. A germinal artist in this regard was Kenneth Anger, who began making intensely personal films in the early 1940s, deploying

classical music in some of his most celebrated works—
Antonio Vivaldi in *Eaux d'artifice* (1953), Leoš Janáček
in *Inauguration of the Pleasure Dome* (1954)—and classic
rock in others.

Chief among the latter films is *Scorpio Rising*, a 1965
minidrama about a motorcycle club engaging in vehicle
upkeep; wild partying; narcissistic posturing with echoes
of Hollywood, the zodiac, neo-Nazism, and pop culture;
and unsafe driving that culminates in a fatal crash. The
soundtrack is a collage of Top 40 tunes ranging from
Ricky Nelson's 1963 "Fools Rush In (Where Angels Fear
to Tread)" and Martha and the Vandellas' 1963 "(Love Is
Like a) Heat Wave" to Ray Charles's 1961 "Hit the Road
Jack" and Bobby Vinton's 1963 "Blue Velvet," anticipat-
ing David Lynch's *Blue Velvet* (1986) by more than two
decades. The songs are often placed in ironic counter-
point to the images, as when Peggy March's 1963 "I Will
Follow Him" accompanies a sequence with religious and
political overtones.

Anger also makes striking use of rock music in the brief
Kustom Kar Kommandos (1970), in which a man polishes
his car to the strains of Bobby Darin's 1959 "Dream Lover,"
and in the marvelous *Rabbit's Moon*, a foray into comme-
dia dell'arte pantomime that exists in an original 1972 version, with such songs as the El Dorados' 1957 "Tears on

My Pillow" and the Flamingos' 1959 "I Only Have Eyes for You," and a reedited 1979 version set entirely to A Raincoat's 1976 "It Came in the Night." Two more Anger films also deserve mention: *Invocation of My Demon Brother* (1969), with a minimalist score created and played on a Moog synthesizer by Mick Jagger, and *Lucifer Rising* (1972), with metallic music composed by Bobby Beausoleil, an imprisoned vestige of the Charles Manson family, after plans for a score by the Led Zeppelin star Jimmy Page failed to pan out. In the two last-named films, rock idioms take on forms as idiosyncratic as those of Anger's distinctively mystical movies.

Bruce Conner was active in many fields, producing significant sculptures, assemblages, collages, light shows, and photographs during his fifty-year career. Although cinema was only one of his artistic outlets, his movies were hugely influential on other nonnarrative filmmakers and also on the music-video aesthetic that gained currency with the rise of MTV in the early 1980s. His first film, *A Movie* (1958), introduced his nonlinear, collage-based approach to cinema, flooding the screen with a kinetic series of found-footage clips (gleaned from newsreels, instructional films, soft-core pornography, and other sources) accompanied by Ottorino Respighi's 1924 composition *Pines of Rome.* That is a classical piece, but Conner turned to the rhythm-and-blues beat of Ray Charles's 1959 "What'd I Say" for the soundtrack of his next film, *Cosmic Ray* (1961), which superimposes nuclear blasts, cartoon animation, and other emphatic footage over the nude body of a dancing woman. The somewhat similar *Breakaway* (1966) has Toni Basil dancing in the nude and singing the title song on the soundtrack.

Other films in which Conner uses rock or pop music include *Permian Strata* (1969), a satire of religious kitsch combining sequences from a low-grade hagiopic with Bob Dylan's 1966 "Rainy Day Women #12 & 35"; *Marilyn Times Five* (1973), which attacks the objectification of women by pairing five monotonous repetitions of a 1940s pornographic clip with Marilyn Monroe's rendition of "I'm Through with Love" as heard in Billy Wilder's comedy *Some Like It Hot* (1959); the 1978 masterpiece *Mongoloid*, an inspired proto–music video making a powerful case against conformity and consumerism through a juxtaposition of Devo's 1977 song—"And he wore a hat / And he had a job / And he brought home the bacon / So that no one knew / He was a mongoloid"—with archetypally American found-footage excerpts; and *America Is Waiting* (1982), a cautionary film about the march toward apocalyptic war set to the David Byrne–Brian Eno song of that title, taken from the 1981 album *My Life in the Bush of Ghosts*, a pioneering venture into the collage-like practice of sampling. Conner was an invaluable participant in the experimental rock-movie scene.

As a movie director, producer, and cinematographer, Andy Warhol is best known for notoriously silent pictures like *Sleep* and *Empire* (both 1964) and for flummoxing the notion of a continuous soundtrack in his two-projector epic *Chelsea Girls* (1966). But starting in 1964 and 1965, when he began collaborating with writers like Ronald Tavel and Chuck Wein and then with the filmmaker Paul Morrissey, sound and dialogue counted as much as imagery in his movies. Early in 1966, he and Morrissey hooked up with the Velvet Underground, an aggressively antitraditional rock group that wanted "to do something revolutionary—to combine avant-garde and rock and roll, to do something symphonic," in the words of the electric-viola virtuoso John Cale, who founded the band with the singer-guitarist Lou Reed, its most famous member (Canosa).

Warhol's growing interest in multimedia art led him to produce a series of events in 1966 and 1967 collectively called the Exploding Plastic Inevitable, and he recruited the Velvets to provide the musical component, attracted by their penchant for dark, transgressive lyrics and pointedly unbeautiful sounds. They began working with the German-born model and singer Christa Paffgen, better known as Nico, when Morrissey decided that the group "needed something beautiful to counteract the screeching ugliness they were trying to sell" (Canosa).

Warhol produced the band's first album, *The Velvet Underground & Nico*, which debuted in March 1967 with a characteristic Warhol image—a shapely banana—on the jacket. Several months earlier, however, a movie called *The Velvet Underground & Nico: A Symphony of Sound* had been shot at Warhol's studio, the Factory, showing the titular musicians doing a loosely strung improvisation that rambles on for about an hour, whereupon the New York City police (or actors playing New York City police) arrive, supposedly in response to a noise complaint, and the session stops.

As in many Warhol productions, the camerawork is somehow static and restless at the same time, complementing and enhancing the same qualities in the purposefully aimless music. In the last few minutes, the camera pulls back to give a rare glimpse of the Factory itself, with Warhol and some of his cohorts (Gerard Malanga, Billy Name, Stephen Shore) milling about. In addition to Reed and Cale, those present in the film include the band's other key members—guitarist Sterling Morrison and drummer Maureen Tucker—and Nico's little boy, Ari Boulogne, fiddling intermittently with maracas.

No one could describe this unique movie more accurately than Morrissey, its director of photography:

This was never meant even as an experiment. It was meant as an item of wallpaper made for use behind the musical group as they set up and tuned their instruments. I had been using five different prints of silent footage, mainly screen tests, for simultaneous projection behind them. This was extremely effective while the music was played but in the long stretches between numbers . . . it was very boring.

I thought of recording the Velvets just making up sounds as they went along to have on film so I could turn both soundtracks up at the same time along with the other three silent films being projected. The cacophonous noise added a lot of energy to these boring sections and sounded a lot like the group itself.

This presentation amounted to "the first mixed media show of its kind," according to Morrissey, who claims that he never again saw "such an interesting one even in this age of super-colossal rock concerts" (Morrissey).

The Velvet Underground & Nico: A Symphony of Sound, seen on its own in the post–Exploding Plastic Inevitable era, is of interest as a look at the Velvet Underground at an early stage; as a glimpse of the Warhol scene at one fleeting moment in early 1966; and definitely as an item of wallpaper, remembering that *musique d'ameublement*, or "furniture music," has an honorable history dating at least as far back as 1917, when the great composer Erik

Satie coined the term. Still and all, admirers of the Velvets will be better served by skipping this incontestably subpar performance and listening to one of their sensational albums.

Turning to the cutting edge of European film, Jean-Luc Godard is a quintessential writer-director of the French New Wave that emerged in the late 1950s and promptly revolutionized world cinema. By the later part of the 1960s, Godard was personally and professionally immersed in radical left-wing politics, determined to create films entirely outside what he perceived as an irretrievably corrupt system of production, distribution, and exhibition that enabled and enriched the soul-killing machinery of hegemonic capitalism. To this end, he joined with Jean-Pierre Gorin in 1968 to found the Dziga-Vertov Group, named after a towering filmmaker of the early Soviet Union and deeply indebted to the theories of Bertolt Brecht, already a powerful undercurrent in Godard's thinking. Although works by the group were usually not signed, some films made during this period (1968–72) did carry Godard's name. One was his ornery contribution to rock 'n' roll cinema, *One Plus One*, which premiered in November 1968 at the London Film Festival under the title *Sympathy for the Devil*, the name of the Rolling Stones song that is refined and recorded as the documentary proceeds.

The title change was perpetrated by Iain Quarrier, one of the film's producers, who felt (no doubt correctly) that its viewership would be enhanced if it were named after the opening track of a Rolling Stones album (*Beggars Banquet*) due for imminent release. Quarrier altered the film's ending along similar lines, freezing one of the concluding images and playing "Sympathy for the Devil" in its entirely on the soundtrack. These actions understandably outraged Godard, who meant the film to be a Marxist-Maoist deconstruction of the labor invisibly embedded in cultural artifacts. It was also a Brechtian essay in interruption and disruption, opening a critical distance between the audience and the culture industry by intercutting long, sinuously filmed shots of the Stones in the studio with stylized sketches involving an agitprop bookstore, Black Panthers in a junkyard, a woman named Eve Democracy (Anne Wiazemski), and a camera crew on a beach. Godard regarded the title *One Plus One* as crucial—it was a slogan of rebellious students during the May 1968 uprising—and playing the completed song could be taken as pandering to the commercial marketplace. When the film opened at the London festival, Godard leapt onto the stage, urged audience members to demand their money back and donate it to the Black Panther–linked Eldridge Cleaver Fund, and pronounced them "bourgeois fascists" if they refused. He then punched Quarrier in the nose (Sarris, "Godard" 53).

Under either title, Godard's film is at once a mesmerizing account of the creation of a truly great rock recording and a confrontational time capsule of what the essayist Tom Wolfe termed "radical chic" at the outset of the 1970s (1). To call it insufferable, infuriating, and cranky is to pay it the kind of compliment Godard was hoping to hear (and did hear) when he made it.

3

THE SLIPPERY 1970s

The 1970s were the decade of Watergate, the unprecedented political scandal that culminated in Richard M. Nixon's resignation from the US presidency on 9 August 1974, and of the withdrawal of US forces from the long, savage, and wearying Vietnam War, prepared by the signing of the Paris Peace Accords on January 27, 1973, and finalized by the fall of Saigon and evacuation of US personnel in late April 1975. These were among the developments that enabled what the cultural scholar Lester D. Friedman calls "a pervasive sense of insecurity [to] spread broadly across the American landscape" (7).

Many events and conditions propelled and exacerbated this insecurity. Among them were economic stagflation, the deadly Attica prison riot in September 1971, the resignation of Vice President Spiro T. Agnew in October 1973 after pleading nolo contendere to bribery and tax-evasion charges, the beginning of the Arab oil embargo in late 1973, the suicidal cataclysm at the Reverend Jim Jones's cult in Guyana in November 1978, and a long line of other events seen by many people as destabilizing, disorienting, or ominous in what they revealed about the present and portended for the future. Even developments that sizable numbers of Americans found welcome and good—the rise of modern feminism, the Supreme Court's momentous *Roe v. Wade* decision curtailing antiabortion laws in 1973, the creation of the cabinet-level Department of Energy by President Jimmy Carter in August 1977—struck others as ill advised or wrong.

Pop-culturally speaking, the 1970s brought the ascent of the hippies, the upsurge of pantsuits and bellbottoms, the premieres of socially aware sitcoms like *All in the Family* (CBS, 1971–83) and its spin-off *The Jeffersons* (CBS, 1975–85), and the beginnings of home-video entertainment via Betamax, placed on the American market by Sony in November 1975. On the musical scene, the Beatles broke up, three top-of-the-line rock stars—Jimi Hendrix, Janis Joplin, and Jim Morrison—all died at age twenty-seven, and Elvis Presley died at forty-two. Soft rock, glam rock, and glitter rock lit up the nights until hard-pumping disco triumphed in the decade's second half, only to be vanquished in turn by the primitive pulse of punk. The best-selling LPs of the 1970s were strikingly heterogeneous, ranging from Simon & Garfunkel's *Bridge over Troubled Water* (1970) and the Rolling Stones' *Sticky Fingers*

(1971) to Pink Floyd's *Dark Side of the Moon* (1973) and the Bee Gees' *Saturday Night Fever* (1978). Eclecticism reigned.

The rock 'n' roll movie scene was less robust in the 1970s than in the previous two decades, for various reasons. The film and album *Let It Be* confirmed the demise of the Beatles; the thrilling Elvis of Nashville and the ambitious Elvis of Hollywood had become the pudgy, pill-popping Presley of Las Vegas; subgenres like the rock documentary and concert film were now established staples rather than nervy newcomers; and although pop music remained an important part of many people's lives, its cachet was inevitably declining after the enormous rush it enjoyed in the 1960s. For sheer fascination, moreover, no rock-movie phenomenon later in the 1970s could top the near-simultaneous arrival of two supremely complementary films—*Woodstock* and *Gimme Shelter*—that premiered a few months apart in the decade's first year, encapsulating and exposing some of the most richly contradictory cross-currents in music culture, youth culture, and American culture at large.

WOODSTOCK AND ALTAMONT

The Woodstock Music and Art Fair, also known as An Aquarian Exposition: 3 Days of Peace and Music, or just Woodstock, took place from August 15 to 17, 1969, on a six-hundred-acre hayfield owned by an upstate New York dairy farmer. I was there, and my reporting on the event read in part,

> It was—suddenly—the third largest city in New York State. . . . Many of the [advance] worries turned out to be fully justified, especially as the crowd grew to a size reportedly four times the number that had been expected.
>
> Serious food and water shortages developed; sanitation facilities proved sadly inadequate; problems with illness were aggravated by the impossibility of moving ambulances through the traffic jams that stretched for miles in all directions. . . .
>
> While no one seemed to have a kind word for the mismanaging entrepreneurs who had caused the rockfest itself and the discomforts it brought, nobody had an unkind word for anyone else. . . .
>
> The concerts themselves materialized much as planned, despite delays, technical problems, and goodly amounts of rain and mud. . . . For three days in a conservative rural community, the generation gap was bridged by people confronting and conquering a unique situation. (Sterritt, "N.Y. Rock Fest")

That was the conventional wisdom in the event's immediate aftermath, and the conventional wisdom was accurate, notwithstanding the contrary view espoused by Barry Melton of Country Joe and the Fish, who said that people praising Woodstock must be talking about the movie, not the festival (Coates). The three-day concert was plagued by rain, mud, overcrowding, and confusion about which drugs circulating through the population were safe, dangerous, or indifferent, but the local citizens were warm and generous in response to a difficult situation for which they hadn't asked and from which they wouldn't profit. Thirty-two acts did their stuff for an audience of some four hundred thousand listeners, and the outcome seemed to confirm the truth of hippie platitudes about the transcendent well-being to be expected in the dawning age of Aquarius.

About seven months after the sprawling three-day festival concluded, a sprawling three-hour concert movie premiered, and a 225-minute director's cut arrived in 1994 to mark the event's twenty-fifth anniversary. *Woodstock: 3 Days of Peace & Music* was directed by Michael Wadleigh, photographed by Wadleigh and several others including Richard Pearce and David Myers, and edited by Wadleigh and several others including Martin Scorsese and Thelma Schoonmaker, who also served as assistant directors. Wadleigh intercuts the musical acts with far more crowd footage, vox-pop interviewing, and atmospheric B-roll than Pennebaker uses in the somewhat similar

Monterey Pop, and he juices up the ambience with a plethora of split-screen effects and aspect-ratio switches that attracted considerable notice when the movie was new; the *New York Times* critic Vincent Canby speculated in his 1970 review that Wadleigh used these devices "to stimulate a feeling of participation on the part of the theater audience" (*"Woodstock"*).

As always in concert films aspiring to variety and inclusiveness, the quality of the performances is varied. Joan Baez sings the 1936 labor-movement song "Joe Hill" and the classic spiritual "Swing Low, Sweet Chariot" in a lovely and restrained set. John Sebastian exudes sincerity in a solo rendition of the Lovin' Spoonful hit "Younger Generation" (1970). Country Joe and the Fish shake things up with their exuberantly antiwar "I-Feel-Like-I'm-Fixin'-to-Die Rag" (1965), the Who give a powerful account of "See Me, Feel Me" (1969) and two other songs, and key superstars of the era—Jefferson Airplane, Joplin, Hendrix—acquit themselves well. Farther down on the quality graph, the retro pop of Sha Na Na seems oddly out of place in these generally psychedelic surroundings, and Arlo Guthrie's performance of "Coming into Los Angeles" reminds one why the remarkable "Alice's Restaurant Massacree" remains the only standout work by this personable but lightweight singer-songwriter. Although the yowling, twitchy version of "With a Little Help from My

Friends" by Joe Cocker and the Grease Band is regarded by some people as a great Woodstock moment, for this observer it is not a highlight but a low point.

A mere four months after the peace and music of the Woodstock lovefest, the darker side of the fading 1960s barged into the pop-culture scene via the Altamont Speedway Free Festival, a one-day event on December 6, 1969, at a California car-racing venue. An estimated three hundred thousand music fans jammed the venue, expecting a Woodstock West with stars like Jefferson Airplane and Santana, who had played at Woodstock, and the Rolling Stones and the Grateful Dead, who had not.

Of the countless things that went wrong in the planning and execution of the event, which the Dead and the Stones had been instrumental to setting in motion, the most disastrous by all accounts was the decision to hire dozens of members of the Hells Angels Motorcycle Club to provide "security" in exchange for $500 worth of beer. Disturbed by the escalating mood of violence as the concert proceeded and daylight waned—among others things, the Jefferson Airplane singer Marty Balin was knocked unconscious by a Hells Angel when he tried to intercede in a fight—the Dead vacated the premises, leaving the Stones to close the show as scheduled. While they were performing their 1966 hit "Under My Thumb," a Hells Angel named Alan Passaro stabbed and killed

Meredith Hunter, a young African American man who pulled a revolver after members of the gang violently hassled him for approaching the stage. Three other deaths, all accidental, occurred as well. Passaro was tried for killing Hunter and acquitted on grounds of self-defense.

"It was perhaps rock and roll's all-time worst day, . . . a day when everything went perfectly wrong," opined *Rolling Stone* two months after the debacle (Burks). The episode entered the annals of film history by way of Maysles Films, which had been accompanying the Stones with a sizable crew (including George Lucas and Walter Murch) on the US tour that climaxed at Altamont. The Maysles crew fortuitously captured the killing of Hunter in several seconds of clear footage taken by three cameras; the principal one was fifteen feet over the stage and about thirty feet from the spot where the stabbing occurred.

The material shot at Altamont became the main pillar of the 1970 documentary *Gimme Shelter*, directed by Albert and David Maysles with Charlotte Zwerin, one of their regular collaborators. The brothers were not new to rock cinema; their earlier films include *What's Happening! The Beatles in the USA*, a rarely screened 1964 feature that exists in more than one version. *Gimme Shelter* includes non-Altamont material as well as footage from that festival, showing the Stones performing in previous concerts and working on their 1971 album *Sticky Fingers* in an

American studio. But the film commences with the killing, as viewed by Mick Jagger and Charlie Watts in rough
footage on an editing machine in the Maysles studio. And
the film circles back to this footage in the end, freezing
frames so that the physical event and its cultural import
are as plain as cinéma-vérité can make them.

As if the fatal ruckus at Altamont weren't enough to
persuade skeptics that the 1960s had come to the bad end
they deserved all along, a number of mainstream cultural
arbiters came down hard on the Maysles film as well,
charging the filmmakers with appropriating and exploit-
ing a murder for the sake of profits and publicity. "The
depressing thing about the movie," Canby wrote in the
New York Times, "is . . . the exuberant opportunism with
which it exploits the events, much as the people within
the movie exploit the Stones (with the Stones [*sic*]
whole-hearted cooperation), and as the Stones exploit
their public" ("Making Murder Pay?" 45). The *New
Yorker* critic Pauline Kael said reviewing *Gimme Shelter*
was comparable to "reviewing the footage of President
Kennedy's assassination or Lee Harvey Oswald's murder." She suggested that the concert was staged in order
to be filmed, just as the 1934 Nazi rally in Nuremberg
had been staged for the benefit of Leni Riefenstahl's 1935
documentary *Triumph of the Will*. Does the documentary
"cinema of fact" remain a valid concept, Kael wondered,

when "the facts are manufactured for the cinema?" She ended her essay by likening the Maysles brothers' depiction of Altamont to "a Roman circus, with a difference: the audience and the victims are indistinguishable" ("Beyond Pirandello" 112)

The facts are different: the Stones' tour was well under way before the Maysles brothers joined them, and the idea of presenting the Stones and other stars in a free post-Woodstock concert hardly depended on the presence of a camera crew to document it. Then, too, accusations of exploitation are all too easy to fire off, as illustrated by the reception of such other important Maysles pictures as *Salesman* (1969, directed with Zwerin) and *Grey Gardens* (1975, directed with Ellen Hovde and Muffie Meyer). *Gimme Shelter* is not immune to critical analysis on this level—like most nonfiction films seeking wide audiences, it arranges its material into a canny structure designed to maximize visual allure, narrative curiosity, and psychological engagement—but it merits full respect as a historical document and a key cultural artifact of its time.

Gimme Shelter is one of many films in which the Direct Cinema ideal pioneered and practiced by David Maysles (until his death in 1987) and Al Maysles (until his death in 2015) has proven its lasting worth. Discussing a shot in which Watts is manifestly discomfited by awareness of the camera's gaze, the film scholar Joe McElhaney writes that like this individual moment, "the film as a whole . . . derives its force from its focused intensity, its rapt fascination with the decadent spectacle of this world, capturing it at the peak of its powers and at a pivotal moment of disintegration" (90). That precisely catches the ongoing value of this unique documentary.

Jagger figures prominently in another 1970 release, *Performance*, a mildly innovative crime drama. Directed by Donald Cammell and Nicolas Roeg in 1968, it was shelved by Warner Bros. for two years before opening to mixed reviews. Jagger makes his acting debut as Turner, a faded rock star whose London house becomes the refuge of the mobster Chas (James Fox) when the latter needs to hide from Harry Flowers (Johnny Shannon), his gangland boss. Plot twists involving psychological manipulation, sexual ambiguity, and a psychedelic mushroom lead to a celebrated climax in which the camera tracks the trajectory of a bullet speeding through Turner's brain. The film invokes the name and face of Argentine author Jorge Luis Borges, whose spirit hovers over the production. Jagger sings "Memo from Turner" in the movie and on the soundtrack album, which also features Randy Newman, Buffy Sainte-Marie, Ry Cooder, Merry Clayton, and Jack Nitzsche's original score.

ZAPPED

A few traditional Hollywood musicals premiered in 1971—Norman Jewison's *Fiddler on the Roof*, Robert Stevenson's *Bedknobs and Broomsticks*, Mel Stuart's *Willy Wonka & the Chocolate Factory*—and Ken Russell shook up the tradition a bit with *The Boy Friend*. But the rock world's most interesting contribution to the year's cinematic output was *200 Motels*, codirected by Frank Zappa, who was in charge of the "characterizations," and Tony Palmer, who handled the "visuals" of the picture. Zappa was well established as the leader, lead guitarist, and lead singer-songwriter of the Mothers of Invention, one of the most resourceful, experimental, and uncategorizable bands of its day, whereas Palmer was a relatively foursquare director of music-centered documentaries for the BBC and other mainstream outlets. Their film was the first theatrical release to be shot on color videotape, then transferred to thirty-five-millimeter film through a process devised by Technicolor's new Vidtronics division.

Alongside his work with the Mothers, which he disbanded in 1969 and regrouped with personnel changes in 1970 and 1973, Zappa conducted a parallel career as a serious composer in the avant-garde tradition of the French trailblazer Edgard Varèse, whom he considered a spiritual mentor, frequently quoting his aphorism, "The present-day composer refuses to die." Zappa's first foray into filmmaking provided a different sort of creative outlet, and *200 Motels* proved as unpredictable as a Mothers album, presenting an impressionistic portrait of a touring rock group enduring the "grueling hours, the seeming sameness of cities hurriedly visited, [and] the banal plasticity of . . . motel rooms," as I described it in my review. In style, the film reflects the interplay between Zappa's antic neo-Dadaism, which introduces spontaneous elements of the sort embraced by John Cage's philosophy of chance-based composition, and Palmer's efforts to impose cinematic order with editing and optical-printing techniques. Noting that it was the first feature ever shot on videotape, I wrote in 1971 that "both the fluidity and the versatility of the tape medium have left a definite mark on the final product." Just as important was Zappa's idea that "all sounds and sight in the movie are part of its 'score,' no matter how gratuitous or careless—perhaps the word should be 'aleatory'—they happen to be." All of which adds up to "Cageian aesthetics [in] a rock 'n' roll movie" (Sterritt, ". . . and Zappa's").

Critics were bemused by *200 Motels*. Roger Ebert wrote that it "is not the kind of movie you have to see more than once. It is the kind of movie you can barely see once: not because it's simple, but because it's so complicated that you finally realize you aren't meant to get everything and sort everything out. It is a full wall of sight-and-sound input, and the experience of the input— not its content[—]is what Zappa's giving us. . . . If there is more that can be done with videotape, I do not want to be there when they do it." *Variety* called the action "often outrageously irreverent" and the comedy "both sophisticated and sophomoric" ("*200 Motels*"). In the *New York Times*, Canby saluted Zappa as "the Orson Welles of the rock world" but found the "initially stunning . . . visual effects" to be "immensely distracting in case you have any interest in the score." While the music "includes some of the most ambitious material ever written by Zappa," he added, it "tends to go into one head and out the other, as if in flight from the almost predatory optical tricks" ("Frank Zappa's").

In sum, Zappa's first film was as provocative, vexing, and eccentric as was his first LP, the groundbreaking Mothers concept album *Freak Out!* from 1966. While the album has gained a reasonably wide following, the movie languishes in unmerited obscurity, although Thorsten Schütte's 2016 documentary *Eat That Question: Frank Zappa in His Own Words* offers a glimpse of the maestro conducting part of the score. Zappa's other directorial credits include a 1988 making-of film, *The True Story of Frank Zappa's 200 Motels*, and assorted documentaries and videos. That said, *200 Motels* remains his cinematic magnum opus.

FRANK AND THE STONES

The mostly traditional musicals of 1972 ranged from Bob Fosse's mildly unconventional *Cabaret* and Peter H. Hunt's comedy-drama *1776* to Arthur Hiller's sentimental *Man of La Mancha* and William Sterling's *Alice's Adventures in Wonderland*, all of which except the last (a British film based on Lewis Carroll's novels) are set in the past and adapted from Broadway stage hits. Moving closer to the rock world, Sidney J. Furie's biopic *Lady Sings the Blues* stars the great soul singer Diana Ross as the great jazz singer Billie Holiday, and the rock-concert genre served up Richard T. Heffron's documentary *Fillmore*, showing Jefferson Airplane, the Grateful Dead, and other bands performing in the last concerts at the eponymous San Francisco auditorium, which was closed in July 1971 by the music promoter Bill Graham, who also appears in the picture, a *Woodstock*-style exercise with split-screen effects galore. Television kicked in with the Liza Minnelli concert movie *Liza with a Z*, an NBC special directed and choreographed by Fosse, and *Imagine*, directed by John Lennon, Yoko Ono, and Steve Gebhardt, who present a televisual blend of fact and fantasy incorporating music by Lennon and Ono (released in a trimmed-down videocassette edition in the 1980s).

The year's most momentous rock-movie event was also its most obscure rock-movie event, for reasons extraneous to the quality of the film itself. From its scurrilous title to its scandalous content, *Cocksucker Blues* pungently captures the more anarchic sides of the Rolling Stones, its stars and chief subjects, and of Robert Frank, the legendary photographer who directed the film with crucial assistance from Danny Seymour, a young photographer (credited as "junkie soundman" for the movie) who tragically vanished in unrelated circumstances a year later. Shot in the cinéma-vérité style characterizing most of Frank's films, *Cocksucker Blues* follows the Stones on their first US tour since the 1969 visit that culminated at Altamont, capturing all manner of behavior and misbehavior— genital sex, oral sex, drug use, and more—along the way. One doesn't usually connect the Rolling Stones with the concept of embarrassment, but the candor of the documentary—photographed in part with cameras scattered around the environment for anyone to use on the spur of the moment—made them sufficiently squeamish to seek and obtain a legal order prohibiting any public showing at which Frank was not personally present, and even those were limited to four per year. Hence the obscurity of *Cocksucker Blues*, although samizdat video copies have long circulated. (In 1966, Peter Whitehead's similarly rough-and-ready documentary *Charlie Is My Darling* had

captured the grit of a Stones tour without the sensational-
istic details that sent Frank's film underground.)

The title song is an off-the-cuff ditty sung by Mick Jagger and Keith Richards near the beginning. Sample: "Oh,
where can I get my cock sucked? / Where can I get my
ass fucked?" In addition to this number, the film's Stones
performances include "Street Fighting Man" (1968),
"Brown Sugar" (1971), and "You Can't Always Get What
You Want" (1973) as well as teamwork with Stevie Wonder on "Uptight (Everything's Alright)" and "(I Can't Get
No) Satisfaction" (both 1965). The offstage shenanigans
are no less interesting, as when Richards and sax player
Bobby Keys drop a TV set off a hotel-room balcony,
doing it with such a businesslike demeanor that you'd
think it was just another item on a checklist of obligatory
rock-star monkeyshines.

Welcoming a rare theatrical showing in 2016, the *New
Yorker* critic Richard Brody made two observations about
Cocksucker Blues worth quoting at length. In the first, he
contrasts the "composed" quality of Frank's photography with the "decomposed" quality of his cinematography, likening the former to a microscope slide, "a single
exemplary and perfectly trimmed slice of existence seized
and frozen," and the latter to "the unbounded flow of life
itself, with the very borders of the frame yielding to the
power of sudden possibilities and wild impulses." In the

second, Brody addresses the film's disreputable side, suggesting that this "poses the Orphic question of just how far an artist can go too far." At a time when artists' private lives are frequently exposed for all to see, he continues, one wonders "whether that scrutiny will have an effect on the kinds of energies that get expressed and embodied in art. The existence—and the suppression—of *Cocksucker Blues* is a primordial moment in this historic shift." Both points are overstated, but they are insightful nonetheless.

Cocksucker Blues is Frank's most lasting contribution to rock 'n' roll cinema apart from *Candy Mountain*, an atmospheric fiction film he codirected with Rudy Wurlitzer from the latter's screenplay, about a young rock musician's odyssey in search of a legendary guitar maker. Kevin J. O'Connor plays the protagonist, and Joe Strummer, Arto Lindsay, Tom Waits, Leon Redbone, and Dr. John are among the musicians he encounters in his quest.

SCORSESE

Flashing back to the 1960s for a moment, Mike Nichols expanded the relationship between movies and music when he placed preexisting Simon & Garfunkel recordings, including their 1965 signature song "The Sound of Silence," onto the soundtrack of *The Graduate*, his instant classic of 1967. (Simon & Garfunkel wrote new material for the film as well, such as "Mrs. Robinson," which was released on disc the following year.) Not long thereafter, Dennis Hopper followed that lead in a major way with *Easy Rider*, his instant classic of 1969. That paradigm-changing motorcycle-across-America road movie reveled in rock and folk-rock, from Steppenwolf's 1968 hits "The Pusher" and "Born to Be Wild" to numbers by Little Eva, the Byrds, the Jimi Hendrix Experience, the Electric Prunes, and the perennially undervalued Holy Modal Rounders, among others. It is impossible to estimate how much of the film's magnetic appeal to late-1960s youth culture was directly attributable to music, but the impact of the cannily assembled soundtrack was certainly enormous.

Martin Scorsese brilliantly picked up on this practice in his 1967 debut feature *Who's That Knocking at My Door*, named after the Genies' hit "Who's That Knocking?" (1959) and punctuated with apposite songs like the Bell Notes' "I've Had It" (1959), Ray Barretto's "El Watusi" (1961), Junior Walker's "Shotgun" (1965), and the Doors' "The End" (1967), all expertly positioned for expressive effect. But flashing now to the 1970s, it was in 1973 that Scorsese raised the device to an all-time-high level in *Mean Streets*, which begins with the Ronettes singing "Be My Baby" (1963) under the opening titles and soars to an early high point when Johnny Boy (Robert De Niro) enters to the beat of the Rolling Stones pounding out their 1968 opus "Jumpin' Jack Flash."

Mean Streets is not a rock 'n' roll movie, but it often sounds like one. The soundtrack rocks with the sounds of the Marvelettes' "Please Mr. Postman" (1961), Little Caesar and the Romans' "Those Oldies but Goodies" (1961), the Shirelles' "I Met Him on a Sunday (Ronde-Ronde)" (1958), and even the Chips' 1956 novelty number "Rubber Biscuit," all precisely right for the positions they occupy. Scorsese repeated his coup in the 1990 gangland drama *Goodfellas*, which contains many vintage hits—the Drifters' "Bells of St. Mary's" (1954), the Moonglows' "Sincerely" (1955), the Cadillacs' "Speedo" (1955), Billy Ward and His Dominoes' "Star Dust" (1957), Johnny Mathis's "It's Not for Me to Say" (1957), the Crystals' "Then He Kissed Me" (1963), the Shangri-Las' "Leader of the Pack" (1964), Cream's "Sunshine of Your Love" (1967), the Who's "Magic Bus" (1968), Muddy Waters's "Mannish Boy" (1955/1968/1977), and more—as well as standard numbers providing sly commentaries on the film's narrative themes, from the "Rags to Riches" crooned by Tony Bennett (1953) at the beginning to the "My Way" snarled by Sid Vicious (1978) at the end.

"Musicians are outlaws," Scorsese told me. "They're a subculture, just like the guys in *Mean Streets*. It doesn't matter if they're jazz musicians of the '40s, or rock

musicians of today. They have their own language and
life-style. I feel at home with that" (Sterritt, "Scorsese").
His commitment to rock 'n' roll runs especially deep; he
changed the reed-playing protagonist of his 1977 musical
drama *New York, New York*, for instance, from a clarinet-
ist in the original screenplay to a tenor saxophonist in the
shooting script, probably because tenor sax is embedded
much more solidly than clarinet in rock-music tradition.
In addition to other fiction films incorporating rock over
the years, Scorsese entered the concert-film arena with
The Last Waltz, a 1978 documentary that shook up the
subgenre in several ways. It was preplanned in detail with
a three-hundred-page shooting script; it was the first concert movie filmed in thirty-five millimeter and the first
recorded on twenty-four tracks, which were processed in
what was then the longest-lasting sound mix ever; it was
staged with elaborate lighting and design effects involving chandeliers from Twentieth Century-Fox and sets
rented from a production of Giuseppe Verdi's 1853 opera
La Traviata; and it was shot by a six-person crew headed
by Vilmos Zsigmond and Laszlo Kovacs, leading figures
in the field.

The focus of *The Last Waltz* is the band called the Band,
which decided to bid farewell to touring with a valedic-
tory concert on Thanksgiving Day of 1976. To some
extent, the movie is about the exhaustion that drove the

Band from the concertizing scene, but mainly it's about their music and the powerful following they built, first as backup musicians for Bob Dylan and then as stars in their own right, commencing with *Music from Big Pink*, their amazing 1968 debut album. Scorsese intercuts their performance with brief interview segments, and in the course of the film it seems that half the world's rock stars also sidle out, from Dylan, Neil Young, and Dr. John to Ringo Starr, Eric Clapton, Muddy Waters, Joni Mitchell, Paul Butterfield, and others, plus the Beat poets Lawrence Ferlinghetti and Michael McClure for changes of pace. It's a sweeping cross section of rock and its roots, all built with knowing irony on the foundation of the Band's exit from the rigors of touring. Referring to the latter, Scorsese's friend and sometime star Liza Minnelli told me she saw *The Last Waltz* as "a mystery story, a murder mystery: You're killing yourself with this crazy life, but you're still making great music! How, and why, do you do it?" (Sterritt, "Scorsese")

Scorsese returned to music with the Rolling Stones picture *Shine a Light* in 2008; the exhaustive documentary *George Harrison: Living in the Material World* in 2011; two major television episodes—the disappointing *Feel Like Going Home*, which opened the PBS series *The Blues* (2003), and the excellent *No Direction Home: Bob Dylan*, shown in the PBS series *American Masters* (1986–present) in 2005—plus a handful of Michael Jackson videos. He is a key contributor to rock 'n' roll cinema.

LUCAS'S GRAFFITI

If there's any truth to the notion that the 1973 tours, albums, and capers of Alice Cooper, the Who, and Led Zeppelin sent a hitherto healthy pop culture into a money-driven death spiral, it helps explain why moviegoers made a headlong flight into the nostalgic days of yesteryear. Their pilot was George Lucas, the obviously gifted but then-unproven filmmaker whose one previous feature, the overambitious science-fiction fable *THX 1138*, had failed to make waves in 1971. If peering into the future was not to the public's taste, Lucas might have reasoned, then peering into the past was certainly worth a try, and rock 'n' roll conjures up the past more effectively than anything since Marcel Proust's immortal madeleine. It's unlikely that Lucas actually did reason thus, since he was already planning the *Star Wars* franchise, a futuristic juggernaut that makes the earnings of his rock 'n' roll picture seem piffling. But in 1973, he put *American Graffiti* onto the cultural turntable and scored a smash, parlaying a modest $777,000 budget into worldwide grosses of $115 million.

Aesthetic quality cannot be measured by profit margins, of course, but decades later, the free-flowing charm of *American Graffiti* still resonates. Credit goes primarily to Lucas, who wrote the screenplay—a lighter-than-air story about a few Southern California friends transitioning from adolescence to adulthood in the summer of 1962—with Gloria Katz and Willard Huyck, and he directed it with such a winning touch that revisiting it makes one wonder anew why he has taken the director's chair for only half a dozen features over the course of his long career. Credit also goes to the casting, which transformed the TV actors Richard Dreyfuss, Ron Howard, and Cindy Williams into movie stars, provided valuable exposure to Charlie Martin Smith, Candy Clark, and Paul Le Mat, and gave disc jockey Wolfman Jack a vivid, if fleeting, screen presence.

Although the narrative is not about music, the characters are exactly the kind of early-1960s teenagers, high-school grads, and hangers-on who would have been steeped in rock 'n' roll radio almost everywhere they spent their discretionary time. *American Graffiti* reproduces the sonic sea in which they swim, packing its soundtrack with some forty-four numbers, fewer than Lucas wanted and lacking Elvis Presley titles that the budget couldn't afford, but plentiful all the same. Some are cover versions performed by Flash Cadillac & the Continental Kids, a minor retro band, but most are authentic classics done by major artists like Fats Domino, Buddy Holly, Frankie

Lymon, the Flamingos, the Platters, the Diamonds, the Del Vikings, Bill Haley and His Comets, Chuck Berry, and the Beach Boys and by lesser lights like Lee Dorsey, Buddy Knox, the Big Bopper, the Regents, and Joey Dee and the Starlighters, to name only some. It's fair to call *American Graffiti* a featherweight amusement with little depth or breadth, but as a pop-culture time capsule, it is a leader of the pack.

Other rock films of 1973 include Mel Stuart's soul-concert movie *Wattstax* and Claude Whatham's musical drama *That'll Be the Day*, starring the actor-singer David Essex as an aspiring pop star and featuring the rockers Ringo Starr and Who drummer Keith Moon in supporting roles. Honorable mention also goes to Terrence Malick's stunning debut film, *Badlands*, in which the runaway outlaws played by Martin Sheen and Sissy Spacek dance to the insinuating beat of Mickey and Sylvia's great 1957 single "Love Is Strange."

1974: THE PHANTOM OF DE PALMA

Before Brian De Palma was the cinematically assured director of horror movies like *Carrie* (1976) and *The Fury* (1978) and thrillers like *Dressed to Kill* (1980) and *The Untouchables* (1987), he was the idiosyncratic auteur of eccentric items like *Greetings* (1968) and *Hi, Mom!* (1970), which make up in whimsy what they lack in consistency and lucidity. His satirical shocker *Phantom of the Paradise* is a transition film, combining the flightiness of his early features with gestures toward the narrative drive and visual pizzazz that flowered in his later work. Although the movie's ambitions fall prey to the sledgehammer stylistics that De Palma deploys in almost every scene, *Phantom of the Paradise* is the most noteworthy rock 'n' roll movie to arrive in 1974. This sums up the generally undistinguished showing of the subgenre in that year.

One of De Palma's favorite actors, William Finley, plays Winslow Leach, a young composer looking desperately for an impresario who'll put on performances of his magnum opus, a cantata based on the Faust legend. Unfortunately for him, the impresario he finds is Swan (Paul Williams), a power-obsessed entrepreneur who steals Winslow's composition and orders his thugs to throw the composer out when he comes looking for payment or at least recognition for his work. Seething with rage, Winslow stumbles into a horrible accident that ruins his voice, disfigures his face so badly that he hides behind a mask, and turns his mind into a one-track vengeance machine. He is now the Phantom of the Paradise, skulking in the shadows of Swan's rock 'n' roll domain. Swan takes advantage of Winslow's addled wits and lures him into a Faustian contract—literally Faustian, signed in blood—whereby Winslow's cantata will be the opening attraction of the Paradise, the fabulous new showplace that Swan is about to open. Subplots involve Swan's own Faustian contract, signed with the Devil himself, and the murderous rivalry between Swan and Winslow over Phoenix (Jessica Harper), a pretty singer who's edged out of the spotlight by Beef (Gerrit Graham), a loudmouthed glam rocker.

The multitalented Williams wrote the movie's score, including numerous songs performed by Finley, Harper, Graham, and himself, plus a shape-shifting trio that portrays three different rock groups called the Juicy Fruits, the Beach Bums, and the Undead. Compounding elements from the Faust mythos, Rupert Julian's fine movie *The Phantom of the Opera* (1925), Oscar Wilde's classic 1890 novel *The Picture of Dorian Gray*, and De Palma's penchant for split screens and visual flimflam, *Phantom of the Paradise* is both a lurid salute and an impertinent middle finger to the glam and glitter scenes that were displaced by both disco and punk before the decade was through.

Michael Apted's drama *Stardust*, about an English rock musician with mental and addiction challenges, also arrived in 1974, along with a double soundtrack album featuring a diverse array of talents ranging from Del Shannon, Derek and the Dominos, the Beach Boys, and Martha Reeves and the Vandellas to Jefferson Airplane, the Box Tops, the Drifters, and of course the Who, who seemed to be everywhere around this time. England's greatest band reappeared in Rollin Binzer's concert documentary *Ladies and Gentlemen: The Rolling Stones*, filmed in sixteen millimeter and thirty-two-track sound (blown up to thirty-five millimeter and mixed in yet another new format, Quadrasound, for theatrical release) during four shows in the group's North American tour promoting their 1972 album *Exile on Main St.* Janis Joplin reappeared as well, still popular enough to draw moviegoers to the Canadian director Howard Alk's archival documentary *Janis* four years after her death in 1970.

1975: ROCK OPERA, POP OPERA

Authorities differ on the origin of the concept album, but the arrivals of the Beach Boys' *Pet Sounds* in 1966, the Beatles' *Sgt. Pepper's Lonely Hearts Club Band* in 1967, and the Who's *Tommy* in 1969 date the format to the second half of the 1960s. *Sgt. Pepper's Lonely Hearts Club Band* was adapted into an uproariously bad movie by Michael Schultz in 1978, but *Tommy* became a lively film, if not a particularly coherent one, in 1973, under the aegis of Ken Russell, whose classical-music biopics—such as the exquisite TV movie *Song of Summer: Frederick Delius* (1968) and the uneven theatrical films *Mahler* (1974) and

The Music Lovers (1970)—paved the way for his daring venture into rock territory.

Tommy began as a 1969 double album written primarily by Pete Townshend, the Who's lead guitarist and chief singer-songwriter; according to David James, this was "the first composition specifically designated as a rock opera" (448), although that was clearly a marketing ploy, since Townshend regarded it as basically a series of single songs, saying, "As a gag, when we were working on it, we started to call it a rock opera knowing full well it wasn't a true opera at all" ("What's Deaf"). After premiering in full-length concerts in 1969, it was adapted into dance by Les Grands Ballets Canadiens in 1971 and into a star-studded London stage extravaganza that spawned a newly recorded version in 1972.

The band was jittery about putting the property into the hands of moviemakers, but ground for such a venture had been prepared in 1973, when two biblically themed pictures based on Broadway shows—David Greene's *Godspell: A Musical Based on the Gospel According to St. Matthew* and Norman Jewison's *Jesus Christ Superstar*—earned good reviews amid mild amounts of controversy from guardians of public religiosity. With this in mind, the Who signed a deal with Robert Stigwood, who had produced *Jesus Christ Superstar* on stage and screen. Stigwood then signed a deal with Columbia Pictures, which agreed to gamble on *Tommy* after all Hollywood's other major studios declined. The members of the Who were encouraged by Russell's reputation as a creative film-maker, and Russell spent a year working on the screenplay with Townshend, who also wrote four new songs, making the score thirty-five minutes longer than the double album. The film is a bona fide opera in the sense that all its words are sung rather than spoken.

Retaining the album's elliptical story line but expanding it with backstory and new characters, the movie focuses on a man who is blind, deaf, and mute as a result of childhood trauma and grows up to be a world pinball champion and then a bogus New Age messiah. The principal cast (Ann-Margret, Oliver Reed, Who lead singer Roger Daltry) and supporting players (Jack Nicholson, Tina Turner, Elton John, Eric Clapton, the other Who members) lip-synched to their own prerecorded singing, which was mixed in Quintaphonic sound, a brand name for quadrophonic sound with an added speaker behind the screen to carry the vocals (Denisoff and Romanowski 214–15). The film garnered Academy Award nominations for Ann-Margret's acting and Townshend's score.

At the same time *Tommy* was being shot, Russell was preparing the screenplay for his next film, *Lisztomania*, which opened just seven months later. This is a more typical Russell production (if there is such a thing) in that it's a musical biography of Franz Liszt, the nineteenth-century Hungarian composer. Russell wanted a rock star to play the lead because he believed Liszt's cult following directly prefigured the rock-star cults of more recent times. He also thought Daltry's physiognomy was virtually identical to that of Liszt, and more broadly, he saw rock musicians as excellent candidates for movie casting, since they have experience in presenting themselves publicly but are not schooled in standard-issue acting techniques. (After casting Michelle Phillips as Natasha Rambova in his 1977 dance biopic *Valentino*, he appeared to have gotten this out of his system.)

Although the score of *Lisztomania* is naturally drawn largely from Liszt, with bits of Richard Wagner here and there, the original music was composed by Rick Wakeman, best known as the keyboardist and songwriter of the progressive rock band Yes, which presented its own likable concert-tour film, *Yessongs*, directed by Peter Neal, in 1974. Wakeman and Daltry both wrote lyrics for numbers in *Lisztomania*, and the cast includes Wakeman as the god Thor and Ringo Starr as the pope.

Jim Sharman built his reputation as a venturesome theater director by staging early productions of two major pop musicals—James Rado, Gerome Ragni, and Galt MacDermot's *Hair: An American Tribal Love-Rock Musical* in 1969 and *Jesus Christ Superstar* in 1972—and in

1973, he directed the first production of Richard O'Brien's horror-comic musical *The Rocky Horror Show*, starring Tim Curry as Dr. Frank N. Furter, a transvestite mad scientist who has created a *Frankenstein*-type creature named Rocky Horror in his laboratory. When a stranded young couple (awful storm, dark road, flat tire) enter his castle, they meet both of those characters as well as Furter's hunchbacked assistant, Riff Raff, and other denizens of the creepy edifice. A great deal of singing, dancing, and sexual horseplay ensue, and at the end, the young couple look on in amazement as the castle rockets into outer space with the surviving inhabitants on board.

Several productions later, Sharman and Curry brought the show to Broadway, where it opened in March 1975 at the Belasco Theater—temporarily renamed the Beautiful Belasco and refitted with cabaret-style tables—but lasted less than a month. By this time, Sharman had directed a film version, *The Rocky Horror Picture Show*, adapted from the stage musical by Sharman and O'Brien and still featuring Curry as the crazy cross-dressing genius. Although the movie made little impression when it first reached the screen, it gained unexpected traction when audiences at midnight showings in New York and elsewhere started participating in a novel way, dressing in costumes from the film, chanting lines of dialogue along with the characters, and mischievously breaking the conventional line separating the spectacle on the screen from the spectators in the auditorium. The sui generis response to *The Rocky Horror Picture Show* did not usher in a widespread or enduring new approach to movie-viewing practices, as some observers thought it might, but playful fans of Sharman's film have carried on the tradition ever since. Like its signature dance, the Time Warp, the film remains a unique phenomenon in the annals of rock 'n' roll cinema.

1976 TO 1977: ROCK CINEMA (MOSTLY) WANES

Musicals along more or less traditional lines continued to issue from Hollywood in the decade's latter years; but the once-triumphant genre was patently out of step with younger audiences, and some specimens in the late 1970s had the ring of desperation, from Bryan Forbes's adaptation of Charles Perrault's often-filmed fantasy *Cinderella*, here called *The Slipper and the Rose: The Story of Cinderella* (1976), to Sidney Lumet's adaptation of L. Frank Baum's often-filmed fantasy *The Wonderful Wizard of Oz*, here called *The Wiz* (1978) and given an all–African American cast. Few people felt the need to see these warmed-over projects, packed with on-screen talent and hummable tunes though they were.

Nor did first-rate rock 'n' roll movies rush in to fill the void. Led Zeppelin's concert film *The Song Remains the Same,* filmed during 1973 shows at Madison Square Garden by Peter Clifton and Joe Massot, and the sub-feature-length performance documentary *The Blank Generation,* showing new-wave acts like Blondie and Talking Heads filmed at the lower-Manhattan bistro CBGB by Ivan Král and Amos Poe, were the most notable entries of 1976. The next year brought Wolfgang Büld's *Punk in London,* documenting what the title indicates via bands like X-Ray Spex and the Clash, and Dwight Hemion's *Elvis in Concert,* a fifty-minute TV special shot during Presley's last tour before his death. In an effort to expand the concert-film genre, the Swedish director Lasse Hallström and the Swedish group ABBA collaborated on the Swedish-Australian production *ABBA the Movie,* a documentary-fiction hybrid wherein a disc jockey's quest for interview time with the band spices up backstage and performance material filmed during their Australian tour of 1977.

Specialty items aside, the big pop-rock movie of 1977 was John Badham's disco-driven *Saturday Night Fever,* propelled by John Travolta's feverish dancing skills and pulsing soundtrack music, much of it written and performed by the Bee Gees, whose "Staying Alive" became one of the era's most infectious hits. The story was adapted by the screenwriter Norman Wexler from Nik Cohn's aptly titled *New York* magazine story "Tribal Rites of the New Saturday Night," published in 1976. Almost twenty years later, Cohn confessed that his supposedly nonfictional report was actually a "fraud" that he had perpetrated by inventing a made-up disco dancer as his central figure (LeDuff), but it's unlikely that the film would have been less popular if this had been known at the time.

In the performance that elevated him from the star of the schoolroom sitcom *Welcome Back, Kotter* (ABC, 1975–79) to genuine movie-star status, Travolta plays Tony Manero, a Brooklyn boy with appurtenances familiar from countless Hollywood melodramas—on the negative end, a dead-end job and a suffocating family; on the semipositive side, boundless energy with no constructive outlet. What separates Tony from his peers is his spectacular gift for dancing. By day, he's "a loser less interesting than the cans of paint he sells," I wrote in 1977, but by night, he's "a strutting body-artist howling primitive joy through the twists and leaps of disco ritual" (Sterritt, "Saga"). Among his dancing partners are Annette (Donna Pescow), who's abandoned by Tony and cruelly treated by his friends, and Stephanie Mangano (Karen Lynn Gorney), who's interested in dancing, not romancing him. Subplots involve rape, gang violence, and assorted forms of youthful alienation.

The slender narrative of *Saturday Night Fever* unfolds mainly in the later scenes. Badham enlivens the rest of it

with nonstop visual bounce, playing up the built-in ten-
sions between characters and settings, thematic depths
and glitzy surfaces, aspirational dreams and ugly actu-
alities. "By furiously jockeying his camera even when
there is little of value to see," my review observed, "by
seeking depth of personality among people with nothing much to offer, he creates the illusion of progress and
three-dimensionality, even when Tony and pals are most
aimlessly butting their hard heads" (Sterritt, "Saga").
The film fared well with most critics and very well with
most audiences, earning more than $237 million on its
$3.5 million budget, quite a box-office achievement. And
the transmutation of the Bee Gees from the inventive
popsters of "New York Mining Disaster 1941" (1967) and
"I Started a Joke" (1968) to the disco divinities of "How
Deep Is Your Love" (1977) and "Night Fever" (1978)
was complete.

1978 TO 1979: ROCK CINEMA REBOUNDS

Rock 'n' roll made a cinematic comeback as the end of the
decade approached, and again John Travolta was in the
thick of things, starring in *Grease*, the highest-grossing
film of 1978. Based on the sporadically amusing Broadway
hit of the same name, the movie takes place in 1956, trad-
ing the grainy poetry of the similarly nostalgic *American*

Graffiti for over-the-top stereotyping, in-your-face sight gags, and large-scale production numbers, some of which are quite imaginative. The loosely glued-together plot looks at life and love among a gaggle of mildly disreputable high-school students, and more than Badham does in *Saturday Night Fever*, first-time director Randal Kleiser uses speed and ostentation as substitutes for stylistic subtlety. Like some other rock 'n' roll movies in 1978—Robert Zemeckis's Beatles-fan odyssey *I Wanna Hold Your Hand*, Robert Klane's disc-jockey dramedy *Thank God It's Friday*, John A. Alonzo's disco-powered *FM*, Schultz's awful *Sgt. Pepper's Lonely Hearts Club Band*—it contains more noise than nuance.

The year also brought such top-flight rock pictures as *The Buddy Holly Story*, *The Last Waltz*, and Floyd Mutrux's marvelous *American Hot Wax*, a biopic of Alan Freed, portraying him as a sort of guru and father figure to an elemental art conceived in exuberance and born in the joys of street-corner music making. More than the many 1950s films in which Freed played himself under his own or another name, Mutrux's treatment shows him to have been a radio innovator who truly cared about the music he played and about the musicians who created it by integrating black sounds and styles into middle-class white culture. Apart from weighing a bit too much for the role, Tim McIntire makes an admirably avuncular Freed, and the on-screen talent includes Chuck Berry, Jerry Lee Lewis, Frankie Ford, and Screamin' Jay Hawkins.

Another 1978 arrival worthy of mention is Bob Dylan's directorial debut, *Renaldo and Clara*, a sprawling mélange of concert material from the Rolling Thunder Revue tour of 1975–76, meandering dialogue scenes, documentary footage of the Rubin "Hurricane" Carter case, poetry read by Allen Ginsberg, and more, totaling almost four hours in its originally released version. The cast includes Ronnie Hawkins as Dylan, Ronee Blakely as his wife, and Joan Baez as a Woman in White, plus Harry Dean Stanton, the folk singer Ramblin' Jack Elliott, and many others. According to Dylan, about a third of it was "improvised," about a third "determined," and about a third "blind luck." He identified the themes as "integrity," "knowing yourself," and "alienation of the inner self against the outer self" (Sterritt, "Renaldo & Clara"). Some of the concert footage is magnificent—the rendition of "Isis" (1976) is as stunning as anything in Dylan's discography—and the film as a whole is at once a shapeless mass and a playful, polymorphous essay in dreamlike illogic and purposeful indeterminacy. As a cult movie par excellence, it is edgy, tantalizing, and not for the faint of heart.

Back in mainstream territory, the veteran B-movie entrepreneur Roger Corman returned to rock in 1979 with *Rock 'n' Roll High School*. Directed by Allan Arkush and an uncredited Joe Dante, it features the Ramones as themselves in the story and as artists on the soundtrack, which resounds with songs whose titles suggest the film's antic nature, from "Blitzkrieg Bop" and "Teenage Lobotomy" to "Pinhead" and "I Wanna Be Sedated." Set in 1980, the narrative pits Ramones fans Riff Randell (P. J. Soles) and Kate Rambeau (Dey Young) against Vince Lombardi High School principal Evelyn Togar (Mary Woronov) in a battle over the right of rock 'n' roll to rule the realm of secondary education. Among others heard in the course of the picture are Chuck Berry, Alice Cooper, Devo, Fleetwood Mac, the Velvet Underground, and Brian Eno. A good time is had by all.

It took until 1979 for Hollywood to come up with Milos Forman's screen adaptation of the 1968 stage hit *Hair*, a nearly plotless entertainment about a young man sidetracked by hippies on his way to military service in the Vietnam War, which was raging when the stage musical premiered but over and done with when the movie version belatedly arrived. The great Twyla Tharp choreographed the dance sequences, which Forman and his editors cut into interestingly sliced-and-diced configurations that contrast with the ensemble-oriented choreography created by Julie Arenal for the stage production. Galt MacDermot's score retains many of the songs—"Aquarius," "Sodomy," "Easy to Be Hard," "Good

Morning Sunshine," and the title tune among them—that propelled the theatrical version.

Another belated arrival was Franc Roddam's first feature film, *Quadrophenia*, a 1979 movie based on the Who's 1973 rock opera, itself set in 1965. The story concerns the trials and travails of a mod seeking status and self-understanding through romance, drugs, and admiration of the Who after seeing them in concert. Pete Townshend composed the album on his own, and most (not all) of its numbers are on the soundtrack (and soundtrack album) of the film, although the movie is a drama rather than a musical and the Who does not appear on-screen. As if to remedy a deficit in that department, 1979 also brought Jeff Stein's documentary *The Kids Are Alright*, comprising Who performance footage and archival material spanning the years from 1964 to 1978. Rounding out the year's rock-movie lineup were Neil Young's *Rust Never Sleeps*, his own filmed record of a concert he'd given recently near San Francisco, and Mark Rydell's *The Rose*, starring Bette Midler as a tormented rock star based (very) loosely on Janis Joplin.

4

FROM THE 1980s TO NOW

The most significant rock-movie development of the 1980s was the birth of the faux rockumentary. Although its roots can be seen in 1960s pictures like *A Hard Day's Night* and *Head*, the subgenre came of age with Rob Reiner's *This Is Spinal Tap* (1984), still among the very best of the breed. Later examples include Tamra Davis's "rapumentary" *CB4* (1993), Sacha Gervasi's amusingly titled *Anvil: The Story of Anvil* (2008), and Akiva Schaffer and Jorma Taccone's *Popstar: Never Stop Stopping* (2016).

Real documentaries continued apace. Punk is the subject of Ulli Lommel's *Blank Generation* (1980) and Penelope Spheeris's *The Decline of Western Civilization* (1981), the first installment of a Los Angeles trilogy that went on to examine the heavy-metal scene in the second chapter (1988) and so-called gutter punk in the third (1998). Rap takes over in Peter Spirer's *Rhyme & Reason* (1997); hip-hop is the focus of *Dave Chappelle's Block Party* (2005), directed by the French filmmaker Michel

Gondry; and the experiences of a rocker with bipolar disorder are explored in Jeff Feuerzeig's *The Devil and Daniel Johnston* (2005). Among the many others, a sampling of titles is enough to suggest their comprehensive range: *Metallica: Some Kind of Monster* (2004) by Joe Berlinger and Bruce Sinofsky; *Madonna: Truth or Dare* (1991) by Alek Keshishian; *End of the Century: The Story of the Ramones* (2003) by Jim Fields and Michael Gramaglia; *Beware of Mr. Baker* (2012), about the drummer Ginger Baker, by Jay Bulger; and *Gimme Danger* (2016), about Iggy Pop, by Jim Jarmusch.

Among concert pictures, Jonathan Demme's *Stop Making Sense* (1984), with David Byrne and Talking Heads, is perhaps the most elegantly shot rock-concert film since *The Last Waltz* a decade earlier. Demme also directed *Neil Young: Heart of Gold*, a 1996 blend of Nashville concert footage and Young's reminiscences. Phil Joanou's *U2: Rattle and Hum* (1988), with the Irish band U2, was gorgeously shot by Jordan Cronenweth and Robert Brinkmann, sometimes in luminous color but mostly in scrumptious black and white. Jarmusch shot *Year of the Horse* (1997), about a 1996 tour by Neil Young and Crazy Horse, in super-eight-millimeter after the commercial failure of his extraordinary western *Dead Man*, for which Young created the music, in 1995. Bringing a novel twist to the subgenre, the Beastie Boys and director Adam Yauch (pseudonymously billed as Nathaniel Hörnblowér) made *Awesome: I Fuckin' Shot That!* (2006) by giving fifty camcorders to audience members and editing selected footage into a ferociously kinetic crowd-sourced montage. Kenny Ortega's *This Is It* (2009) documents Michael Jackson's preparations for an upcoming tour that never happened because of the superstar's untimely death. Et cetera.

Rock began to play a significant role in animated cinema in the 1980s, following up the promise of *Yellow Submarine* many years later. The most notable entry was Ralph Bakshi's *American Pop* (1981), a savvy musical drama in which the generations of a Russian-Jewish immigrant family trace the evolution of pop music over several key decades. Herman's Hermits member Keith Hopwood did the music for the 1983 version of *The Wind in the Willows*, directed by Mark Hall and Chris Taylor, and Lou Reed, Iggy Pop, and Deborah Harry are among those heard on the soundtrack of Clive A. Smith's animated Canadian fantasy *Rock & Rule* (1983). Another inventive item was the live-action-plus-animation hybrid *Pink Floyd the Wall* (1982), the story of a mentally disturbed rock musician directed by the ever-versatile Alan Parker and based on the Pink Floyd album released two years earlier.

Last but the opposite of least, rock biopics continued to enrich the movie scene as the twentieth century gave way to the twenty-first. Among the most noteworthy are Alex Cox's harrowing *Sid and Nancy* (1986), galvanized by Gary Oldman and Chloe Webb as Sex Pistols star Sid Vicious and his girlfriend, Nancy Spungen; Oliver Stone's *The Doors* (1991), with Val Kilmer as Jim Morrison, lead singer of the eponymous band; Brian Gibson's *What's Love Got to Do with It* (1993), a superbly directed drama about Ike and Tina Turner, brilliantly played by Laurence Fishburne and Angela Bassett; Michael Winterbottom's *24 Hour Party People* (2002), cleverly recounting a decade and a half in the career of Tony Wilson (Steve Coogan), an English impresario, media personality, and recording entrepreneur; Taylor Hackford's *Ray* (2004), with Jamie Foxx's flawless portrayal of Ray Charles; Gus Van Sant's daringly minimalist *Last Days* (2005), based on the death of Nirvana singer-songwriter-guitarist Kurt Cobain; Todd Haynes's postmodern Bob Dylan epic *I'm Not There* (2007), which is flawed by the same overambitious reach as *Velvet Goldmine* (1998), Haynes's fiction film about a glam rocker; James Mangold's *Walk the Line* (2005), with Joaquin Phoenix as Johnny Cash; Anton Corbijn's *Control* (2007), a thoroughly intriguing study of Joy Division leader Ian Curtis; Bill Pohlad's *Love & Mercy* (2014), about Beach Boys mainstay Brian Wilson, portrayed at two periods of his career by Paul Dano and John Cusack; and F. Gary Gray's *Straight Outta Compton* (2015), tracing the hip-hop career of NWA over a ten-year period starting in the middle 1980s.

EPILOGUE
The Hits Just Keep on Coming

Rock 'n' roll has been evolving, maturing, backsliding, losing its way, leaping ahead, and eluding expected patterns, predilections, and predictions ever since it emerged from the loamy soil of jazz, blues, and rhythm and blues many decades ago. Rock 'n' roll movies have kept pace with the ever-mercurial scene, shifting styles and adjusting subgenres and sub-subgenres in an ongoing dialogue with the music that inspires them.

Looking to the future, all that's certain is that Danny & the Juniors told only half the story back in 1958. "Rock 'n' roll is here to stay, it will never die," they sang; "it was meant to be that way, though I don't know why." They were correct about the seeming immortality of the music, but as for the *why* of it, the answer is plain: simply put, rock 'n' roll is a social force as vital, protean, and unquenchable as modern pop culture itself. Although its tunes, tempos, and lyrics will keep a-changin' with the times, what Chuck Berry hailed as the "backbeat you can't lose" will continue to thrive, as will the cinematic works that capture, crystallize, and circulate the infectious sounds and their limitless sociocultural implications.

FURTHER READING

Aquila, Richard. *That Old-Time Rock & Roll: A Chronicle of an Era, 1954–1963*. Urbana: U of Illinois P, 2000.

Campbell, Michael, with James Brody. *Rock and Roll: An Introduction*. Belmont, CA: Thomson Schirmer, 2008.

Crenshaw, Marshall. *Hollywood Rock: A Guide to Rock 'n' Roll in the Movies*. London: Plexus, 1994.

Denisoff, R. Serge, and William D. Romanowski. *Risky Business: Rock in Film*. New Brunswick, NJ: Transaction, 1990.

Doherty, Thomas. *Teenagers and Teenpics: The Juvenilization of American Movies in the 1950s*. Rev. ed. Philadelphia: Temple UP, 2002.

Driscoll, Catherine. *Teen Film: A Critical Introduction*. New York: Berg, 2011.

Evans, Jeff. *Rock and Pop on British TV*. London: Omnibus, 2017.

Fuchs, Otto. *Bill Haley: The Father of Rock & Roll*. Gelnhausen, Germany: Wagner Verlag, 2011.

Hajdu, David. *Love for Sale: Pop Music in America*. New York: Farrar, Straus and Giroux, 2016.

Hamilton, Jack. *Just around Midnight: Rock and Roll and the Racial Imagination*. Cambridge, MA: Harvard UP, 2016.

Ingham, Chris. *The Rough Guide to the Beatles*. London: Rough Guides, 2003.

James, David E. *Rock 'n' Film: Cinema's Dance with Popular Culture*. New York: Oxford UP, 2015.

Kubernik, Harvey. *Hollywood Shack Job: Rock Music in Film and on Your Screen*. Albuquerque: U of New Mexico P, 2006.

Lewis, Jon. *The Road to Romance and Ruin: Teen Films and Youth Culture*. London: Routledge, 1992.

Muir, John Kenneth. *The Rock & Roll Film Encyclopedia*. New York: Applause Theatre & Cinema Books, 2007.

Romanowski, William D. *Pop Culture Wars: Religion and the Role of Entertainment in American Life*. Eugene, OR: Wipf and Stock, 1996.

Shary, Timothy. *Teen Movies: American Youth on Screen*. London: Wallflower/Columbia UP, 2005.

Welch, Rosanne. *Why "The Monkees" Matter: Teenagers, Television, and American Pop Culture*. Jefferson, NC: McFarland, 2016.

WORKS CITED

Aquila, Richard. *That Old-Time Rock & Roll: A Chronicle of an Era, 1954–1963*. Urbana: U of Illinois P, 2000.

Beatles, The. *The Beatles Anthology*. San Francisco: Chronicle Books, 2000.

Brody, Richard. "*Cocksucker Blues*: Robert Frank's Suppressed Rolling Stones Documentary Comes to Film Forum." *New Yorker* 20 July 2016. http://www.newyorker.com/culture/richard-brody/cocksucker-blues-robert-franks-suppressed-rolling-stones-documentary-comes-to-film-forum.

Burks, John. "Rock & Roll's Worst Day." *Rolling Stone* 7 Feb. 1970. https://web.archive.org/web/20080314073233/http://www.rollingstone.com/news/story/5934386/rock__rolls_worst_day.

Campbell, Michael, with James Brody. *Rock and Roll: An Introduction*. Belmont, CA, Thomson Schirmer, 2008.

Canby, Vincent. "Frank Zappa's Surrealist *200 Motels*." *New York Times* 11 Nov. 1971. http://www.nytimes.com/movie/review?res=9E03E3DA163DEF34BC4952DFB767838A669EDE.

———. "Making Murder Pay?" *New York Times* 13 Dec. 1970: 3, 45.

Canby, Vincent. "*Woodstock*." *New York Times* 27 Mar. 1970. http://www.nytimes.com/movie/review?res= EE05E7DF1738E574BC4F51DFB566838B669EDE.

Canosa, Sandra. "The Factory Factor: Andy Warhol and the Velvet Underground." *Highbrow Magazine* 6 Mar. 2016. http://www.highbrowmagazine.com/5652-factory -factor-andy-warhol-and-velvet-underground.

"Chase & Superchase." *Time* 3 Sept. 1965. http://content.time .com/time/subscriber/article/0,33009,842079,00.html.

Coates, Norma. "*Gimme Shelter* (1970/2000): Blame Wood-stock." *PopMatters* 13 Jan. 2010. http://www.popmatters .com/review/gimme-shelter/.

Cohn, Nik. "Tribal Rites of the New Saturday Night." *New York* 7 June 1976. http://nymag.com/nightlife/ features/45933/.

Crenshaw, Marshall. *Hollywood Rock: A Guide to Rock 'n' Roll in the Movies.* London: Plexus, 1994.

Crowther, Bosley. "The Four Beatles in *A Hard Day's Night*: British Singers Make Debut as Film Stars: A Lively Spoof of the Craze They Set Off." *New York Times* 12 Aug. 1964. http://www.nytimes.com/movie/review?res= 990DE7DE1E30E033A25751C1A96E9C946591D6CF.

———. "Singers Romp through Comic Adventures." *New York Times* 24 Aug. 1965. http://www.nytimes.com/ movie/review?res=9B0CEEDC103CE733A25757C2A96 E9C946491D6CF.

Deming, Mark. "The Monkees." *AllMusic.* 12 Feb. 2017 http://www.allmusic.com/artist/the-monkees-mn0000 478603/biography.

Denisoff, R. Serge, and William D. Romanowski. *Risky Business: Rock in Film*. New Brunswick, NJ: Transaction, 1990.

Doherty, Thomas. *Teenagers and Teenpics: The Juvenilization of American Movies in the 1950s*. Rev ed. Philadelphia: Temple UP, 2002.

Ebert, Roger. "*200 Motels*." *Chicago Sun-Times* 29 Nov. 1971. http://www.rogerebert.com/reviews/200-motels-1971.

Everett, Anna. "1961: Movies and Civil Rights." *American Cinema of the 1960s: Themes and Variations*. Ed. Barry Keith Grant. New Brunswick, NJ: Rutgers UP, 2008. 44–66.

Fear, David. "Inside Criterion's Incredible Restoration of Dylan Doc *Don't Look Back*." *Rolling Stone* 27 Nov. 2015. http://www.rollingstone.com/movies/news/inside-the-restoration-of-dont-look-back-20151127.

Feeney, Mark. "Elvis Movies." *American Scholar* 70.1 (Winter 2001): 53–60.

Friedman, Lester D. "Introduction: Movies and the 1970s." *American Cinema of the 1970s: Themes and Variations*. Ed. Lester D. Friedman. New Brunswick, NJ: Rutgers UP, 2007. 1–23.

Fuchs, Otto. *Bill Haley: The Father of Rock & Roll*. Gelnhausen, Germany: Wagner Verlag, 2011.

Greene, Andy. "Davy Jones: The Life of a Monkee." *Rolling Stone* 29 Mar. 2012. http://www.rollingstone.com/music/news/davy-jones-the-life-of-a-monkee-20120329.

Hollinger, Hy. "Controversial Pic Backfire." *Variety* 14 Sept. 1956: 5.

Ingham, Chris. *The Rough Guide to the Beatles*. London: Rough Guides, 2003.

James, David E. *Rock 'n' Film: Cinema's Dance with Popular Culture*. New York: Oxford UP, 2015.

Kael, Pauline. "Beyond Pirandello." *New Yorker* 19 Dec. 1970: 112–15.

———. "*Having a Wild Weekend*." *New Yorker* 28 July 1980: 17.

Kashner, Sam. "Making Beatlemania: *A Hard Day's Night* at 50." *Vanity Fair* 2 July 2014. http://www.vanityfair.com/hollywood/2014/07/a-hard-days-night-making-of.

Kauffmann, Stanley. "Flying, East and West." *New Republic* 25 Dec. 2000: 22.

LeDuff, Charlie. "Saturday Night Fever: The Life." *New York Times* 9 June 1996. http://www.nytimes.com/1996/06/09/nyregion/saturday-night-fever-the-life.html.

"*Let It Be*." *Variety* 31 Dec. 1969. http://variety.com/1969/film/reviews/let-it-be-1200422185/.

MacDonald, Dwight. *On Movies*. New York: Da Capo, 1981.

McElhaney, Joe. *Albert Maysles*. Urbana: U of Illinois P, 2009.

Mendelsohn, John. "The Beatles: *Let It Be*." *Rolling Stone* 11 June 1970. http://www.rollingstone.com/music/albumreviews/let-it-be-19700611.

Morrissey, Paul. "The Velvet Underground and Nico (A Symphony of Sound)." *Nico Web Site*. 11 Mar. 2017 http://smironne.free.fr/NICO/FILMS/sym.html.

Palmer, Tony. "From the *Observer* Archive, 24 May 1970: The Beatles' Let It Be Is a Bore. Thank Heavens for the Music." *Observer* 24 May 2014. https://www

.theguardian.com/news/2014/may/25/from-observer
-archive-beatles-let-it-be-film.

Partridge, Kenneth. "The Beatles' *Let It Be* at 45: Classic
Track-by-Track Album Review." *Billboard* 8 May 2015.
http://www.billboard.com/articles/review/6561045/
beatles-let-it-be-track-by-track-album-review.

Puterbaugh, Parke. "The British Invasion: From the Beatles
to the Stones, The Sixties Belonged to Britain." *Rolling
Stone* 14 July 1988. http://www.rollingstone.com/music/
news/the-british-invasion-from-the-beatles-to-the
-stones-the-sixties-belonged-to-britain-19880714.

Romanowski, William D. *Pop Culture Wars: Religion and
the Role of Entertainment in American Life*. Eugene, OR:
Wipf and Stock, 1996.

Sarris, Andrew. *The American Cinema: Directors and Directions, 1929–1968*. New York: Da Capo, 1996.

———. "Godard and the Revolution." *Village Voice* 30 Apr.
1970: 53, 61, 63–4. Sarris is quoting a press release from
New Line Cinema, the US distributor of *Sympathy
for the Devil* aka *One Plus One*. Reprinted in *Jean-Luc
Godard: Interviews*. Ed. David Sterritt. Jackson: UP of
Mississippi, 1998. 50–58.

———. "*A Hard Day's Night*." *Read the Beatles: Classic and
New Writings on the Beatles, Their Legacy, and Why They
Still Matter*. Ed. June Skinner Sawyers. New York: Pen-
guin, 2006. Originally published in *Village Voice* 27 Aug.
1964: 56–59.

Schonberg, Edith. "You Can't Fool Public, Says Haley."
Down Beat 30 May 1956: 10.

Stafford, Jeff. "Rock Around the Clock (1956)." *Turner Classic Movies.* 12 Feb. 2017 http://www.tcm.com/tcmdb/title/88497/Rock-Around-the-Clock/articles.html.

Sterritt, David. ". . . and Zappa's Surreal Look at Rock 'n' Touring." *Christian Science Monitor* 1 Dec. 1971: 16.

———. "The Dylan Scene on Film." *Christian Science Monitor* 15 Sept. 1967: 6.

———. "N.Y. Rock Fest Amplifies Goodwill." *Christian Science Monitor* 19 Aug. 1969: 10.

———. "Pennebaker: Not Just 'a Perfect Picture.'" *Christian Science Monitor* 17 May 1969: 6.

———. "Renaldo & Clara Meet John Cage: Aleatory Cinema and the Aesthetics of Incompetence." *Senses of Cinema* 5 (Apr. 2000). http://sensesofcinema.com/2000/society-for-cinema-studies-conference-2000/renaldo/.

———. "Saga of a Brooklyn Disco Dancer." *Christian Science Monitor* 21 Dec. 1977: 18.

———. "Scorsese Makes Offbeat Films." *Christian Science Monitor* 1 May 1978: 27.

"200 Motels." *Variety* 31 Dec. 1970. http://variety.com/1970/film/reviews/200-motels-1200422560/.

Walker, Alexander. *Hollywood U.K.: The British Film Industry in the 1960s.* New York: Stein and Day, 1974.

Welch, Rosanne. *Why "The Monkees" Matter: Teenagers, Television, and American Pop Culture.* Jefferson, NC: McFarland, 2016.

"What's Deaf, Dumb & Blind and Costs $3.5 Million? Tommy!" *Rolling Stone* 10 Apr. 1975: 44.

White, Armond. "*Monterey Pop:* People in Motion." *Current* 22 Sept. 2009. https://www.criterion.com/current/posts/235-monterey-pop-people-in-motion.

Wolfe, Tom. *Radical Chic and Mau-Mauing the Flak Catchers*. New York: Farrar, Straus and Giroux, 1970.

INDEX

ABOUT THE AUTHOR

David Sterritt is editor in chief of *Quarterly Review of Film and Video*, contributing writer at *Cineaste*, adjunct professor at the Maryland Institute College of Art, professor emeritus at Long Island University, and past chair of the New York Film Critics Circle and the National Society of Film Critics. His previous publications include *The Films of Alfred Hitchcock* (1993); *Jean-Luc Godard: Interviews* (editor, 1998); *Mad to Be Saved: The Beats, the '50s, and Film* (1998); *The Films of Jean-Luc Godard: Seeing the Invisible* (1999); *Robert Altman: Interviews* (editor, 2000); *Terry Gilliam: Interviews* (coeditor with Lucille Rhodes, 2004); *Screening the Beats: Media Culture and Beat Sensibility* (2004); *Guiltless Pleasures: A David Sterritt Film Reader* (2005); *The B List: The National Society of Film Critics on the Low-Budget Beauties, Genre-Bending Mavericks, and Cult Classics We Love* (coeditor with John Anderson, 2008); *The Honeymooners* (2009); *Spike Lee's America* (2013); *The Beats: A Very Short Introduction* (2015); *The Cinema of Clint Eastwood: Chronicles of America* (2014); and *Simply Hitchcock* (forthcoming 2017).